REDISCOVERING
Aquinas
AND THE SACRAMENTS
STUDIES IN SACRAMENTAL THEOLOGY

REDISCOVERING
Aquinas
AND THE SACRAMENTS
STUDIES IN SACRAMENTAL THEOLOGY

Matthew Levering
Michael Dauphinais
Editors

HillenbrandBooks

Chicago / Mundelein, Illinois

Chapter 5, "Christian Satisfaction and Sacramental Reconciliation" by Romanus Cessario, OP, previously appeared in *Communio* 16 (1989): 186–96. Reprinted with permission of the author.

REDISCOVERING AQUINAS AND THE SACRAMENTS: STUDIES IN SACRAMENTAL THEOLOGY © 2009 Archdiocese of Chicago: Liturgy Training Publications, 3949 South Racine Avenue, Chicago IL 60609; 1-800-933-1800, fax 1-800-933-7094, e-mail orders@ltp.org. All rights reserved. See our Web site at www.LTP.org.

Hillenbrand Books is an imprint of Liturgy Training Publications (LTP) and the Liturgical Institute at the University of Saint Mary of the Lake (USML). The imprint is focused on contemporary and classical theological thought concerning the liturgy of the Catholic Church. Available at bookstores everywhere, through LTP by calling 1-800-933-1800, or visiting www.LTP.org. Further information about the **Hillenbrand Books** publishing program is available from the University of Saint Mary of the Lake/ Mundelein Seminary, 1000 East Maple Avenue, Mundelein, IL 60060 (847-837-4542), on the Web at www.usml.edu/liturgicalinstitute, or e-mail litinst@usml.edu.

Cover photo © The Crosiers/Gene Plaisted, OSC

Printed in the United States of America.

Library of Congress Control Number: 2009931601

ISBN 978-1-59525-032-2

HRAS

Contents

Introduction

In his *The Reenchantment of Nature: The Denial of Religion and the Ecological Crisis*, the evangelical theologian Alister McGrath argues that in order to avoid exploiting or romanticizing nature, "Christians of the twenty-first century need to rediscover the wisdom of earlier generations, which lived out their faith in close contact with the earth."[1] As models of such wisdom, McGrath points to "the monastic traditions of the Egyptian and Syrian deserts in the fourth century, the Celtic Christian approach to nature of the seventh and eighth centuries, the Franciscan love for the natural order of the thirteenth and fourteenth centuries."[2] He praises these Christian communities for being "firmly rooted in the Bible and sensitive to the world around them— a world that was seen and respected as a means of sustaining human life in the present and of reminding and reassuring believers of their future destiny in a renewed creation."[3] Taught by these past Christians, believers today can reclaim an understanding of nature "as a sign and promise of the coming glory of God, its creator."[4] This understanding of nature as "a sign and promise" recalls a central element in the faith of these fourth-century, eighth-century, and thirteenth- and fourteenth-century believers—an element not mentioned by McGrath, but one that would strengthen his case—namely, their faith that God comes to meet us in the sacraments of the new covenant.

The first Christians were already meditating upon this reality of sacramental participation in Christ. Saint Paul rejoices, "Do you not know that all of us who have been baptized into Christ Jesus were baptized into his death? We were buried therefore with him by baptism into death, so that as Christ was raised from the dead by the glory of the Father, we too might walk in newness of life" (Romans 6:4).

---

1. Alister McGrath, *The Reenchantment of Nature: The Denial of Religion and the Ecological Crisis* (New York: Doubleday, 2002), 184.

2. Ibid.

3. Ibid.

4. Ibid., 185.

Water here becomes, mysteriously, an efficacious sign of the new creation. Similarly, Paul asks the Corinthians, "The cup of blessing which we bless, is it not a participation in the blood of Christ? The bread which we break, is it not a participation in the body of Christ? Because there is one bread, we who are many are one body, for we all partake of the one bread" (1 Corinthians 10:16–17). Bread, too, signifies our real participation in Christ's body.

The importance of sacramental signs becomes further evident in the early Church fathers. Thus the early second-century bishop Ignatius of Antioch urges the Ephesians "to obey your bishop and clergy with undivided minds and to share in the one common breaking of bread—the medicine of immortality, and the sovereign remedy by which we escape death and live in Jesus Christ for evermore."[5] Another bishop, Cyril of Jerusalem (mid-fourth century), expresses awe regarding God's action in the sacramental sign of Baptism: "O strange and incomprehensible thing! We did not really die, we were not really buried, we were not really crucified and raised again, but our imitation was but a figure, while our salvation is a reality."[6] Contrasting Christian Baptism with John the Baptist's baptism, Cyril reflects theologically upon Baptism as a sign or "figure" through which the Holy Spirit makes Christ's life, death, and Resurrection present in us. As Cyril says, "Let no one then suppose that Baptism is merely the grace of remission of sins, or further, that of adoption; as John's baptism bestowed only the remission of sins. Nay we know full well, that as it purges our sins, and conveys to us the gift of the Holy Spirit, so also it is the counterpart of Christ's sufferings."[7] Baptism does not merely represent what Christ has done for us; it changes us by configuring us to Christ.[8] This change is sealed by what Cyril calls "the Mystical Chrism."[9] This chrism, says Cyril, is not mere chrism, but rather becomes a sacramental sign that causes the presence

---

5. Ignatius of Antioch, "Epistle to the Ephesians," § 20, in *Early Christian Writings: The Apostolic Fathers*, trans. Maxwell Staniforth, the Rev. Andrew Louth (New York: Penguin, 1987), 66.

6. Cyril of Jerusalem, "Mystagogical Catechesis," II, § 5, in idem, *Lectures on the Christian Sacraments*, trans. R. W. Church, ed. F. L. Cross (Crestwood, NY: St. Vladimir's Seminary Press, 1977), 61.

7. Ibid., 62.

8. Cf. Cyril's "Mystagogical Catechesis," III, § 1, in *Lectures on the Christian Sacraments*, 63.

9. Ibid., § 4, 66.

of the Holy Spirit in us. He compares this sacramental sign to the sign of the Eucharist: "But beware of supposing this to be plain ointment. For as the Bread of the Eucharist, after the invocation of the Holy Spirit, is mere bread no long, but the Body of Christ, so also this holy ointment is no more simple ointment, nor (so to say) common, after the invocation, but the gift of Christ; and by the presence of His Godhead, it causes in us the Holy Spirit."[10]

No less than the other mysteries of faith, therefore, the sacramental mysteries revealed in the New Testament and in the practice of the early Church were joyfully contemplated by those who shared in them. Not surprisingly, Pope John Paul II's encyclical on the Eucharist, *Ecclesia de Eucharistia*, encourages such contemplation and awe: "I would like to rekindle this Eucharistic 'amazement' by the present Encyclical Letter. . . . To contemplate the face of Christ, and to contemplate it with Mary, is the 'program' which I have set before the Church at the dawn of the third millennium, summoning her to put out into the deep on the sea of history with the enthusiasm of the new evangelization" (§ 6). Likewise, Pope Benedict XVI, in his apostolic exhortation *Sacramentum Caritatis*, begins by observing, "What amazement must the Apostles have felt in witnessing what the Lord did and said during that Supper! What wonder must the eucharistic mystery also awaken in our own hearts!" (§ 1).

This amazement, wonder, and contemplative spirit inspired Saint Thomas Aquinas's theological and pastoral writings on the sacraments. John Paul II speaks of Aquinas as "an eminent theologian and an impassioned poet of Christ in the Eucharist" (*Ecclesia de Eucharistia*, § 62), and contemplation is the very goal of Aquinas's *Summa*. Should one expect Aquinas's contemplative insights into the sacraments of the Church, however, to instruct believers today? On the one hand, this question suggests a certain historical naiveté. There is no doubt that Aquinas's sacramental theology—which draws so heavily upon scripture, the Latin and Greek fathers, and the Church's magisterial, liturgical, and canonical tradition—was taken up into the Church's explication of her sacramental faith in the centuries after his death, up to and including the present day. Without learning the rudiments of Aquinas's sacramental theology, students will have

---

10. Ibid, § 3, 65.

much more difficulty understanding the contemporary Church's sacramental theology.

On the other hand, one may also observe that Aquinas's sacramental theology is not particularly well represented today in theological formation. The inquiry into sacramental causality that marks Aquinas's theology, and that we noted above in Cyril of Jerusalem's sacramental theology, can seem overly Aristotelian. Likewise, Aquinas's insistence (with Ignatius of Antioch and Cyril) on the particularity of the Christian sacraments, their exalted character as modes of the Holy Spirit's presence, runs up against certain notions of "sacramentality" that purport to be broader in salvific scope—overlooking the relationship of particular and universal in the Incarnation. Furthermore, some theologians assume that medieval theology, and its descendents up until the Second Vatican Council, possessed a dry, rationalistic, and legalistic view of Christianity, including the sacraments.

In this context, a new introduction to Saint Thomas Aquinas's sacramental theology is needed. Discussing the Thomistic sacramental theology of the early twentieth-century Benedictine Anscar Vonier, Aidan Nichols notes that Vonier exemplifies "how rigorous—and yet religiously exhilarating—the best Catholic theology can be."[11] Regarding Saint Thomas Aquinas himself, Jean-Pierre Torrell remarks, "The figure who at times seems to be known only for his philosophy is also first and foremost a theologian, a commentator on Sacred Scripture, an attentive student of the Fathers of the Church, and a man concerned about the spiritual and pastoral repercussions of his teaching."[12] Is this true about Aquinas's sacramental theology? Do we find in his sacramental theology a concern for its "spiritual and pastoral repercussions"? Is his sacramental theology not only "rigorous," but also "religiously exhilarating," as befits contemplation of the sacramental mysteries?

In light of such questions, this book offers a brief and readable chapter on each of the seven sacraments as presented by Saint Thomas Aquinas, in addition to chapters on his theology of worship and his

---

11. Aidan Nichols, OP, "Introduction" to Anscar Vonier, OSB, *A Key to the Doctrine of the Eucharist* (1925; Bethesda, MD: Zaccheus Press, 2003), xiv.

12. Jean-Pierre Torrell, OP, *Saint Thomas Aquinas*, vol. 2, *Spiritual Master*, trans. Robert Royal (Washington, DC: The Catholic University of America Press, 2003), vii.

understanding of liturgical devotion. The chapters seek to engage students, scholars, and pastors who seek to learn more about Aquinas's sacramental theology. By no means are the chapters intended to be exhaustive or to cover every aspect of each sacrament. Instead, each chapter introduces certain aspects of Aquinas's approach and opens up avenues for further reflection.

Avery Cardinal Dulles's penetrating survey of Saint Thomas's theology of worship serves as an introduction to many of the topics of the volume. Dulles explores the key elements of the virtue of religion—what human beings owe in gratitude to the creator—including adoration, veneration, devotion, prayer, reverence, sacrifice, sacrament, and consecration. He then turns to the Church and the seven sacraments, and sets forth their constitutive elements, as well as Aquinas's teaching on the liturgical rites for the celebration of the sacraments. Dulles concludes that "Saint Thomas remains a valuable resource for situating worship within a theocentric, Christological, and ecclesial framework."

Drawing upon both the *Summa Theologiae* and Aquinas's *Commentary on the Gospel of John*, Michael Dauphinais examines the sacrament of Baptism. Aquinas considers Baptism to be the "door of the sacraments," but Dauphinais points out that a door is generally extrinsic to what lies inside. Contemporary theologians have expressed concern about Aquinas's theology of Baptism on the grounds that his metaphysical rather than experiential approach remains extrinsic to the reality of Baptism. In fact, as Dauphinais emphasizes, Aquinas's metaphysical affirmations about Baptism enable him to illumine how Baptism, as a new creation of the baptized person, suffuses the entirety of the person's life. Furthermore, because the cause of this new creation is Christ's Incarnation and Passion, Aquinas's theology of Baptism avoids individualism: each baptized person is incorporated into the Body of Christ. This metaphysical and individual/communal understanding of spiritual regeneration informs Aquinas's account of the encounter of Nicodemus and Jesus in John 3.

Robert C. Miner's discussion of the sacrament of Confirmation begins with the experience of many teenagers who received this sac-rament and then drift away from the Church during their high school and college years. Is Confirmation perhaps not very important? Recalling that Martin Luther held that Confirmation was not a sacrament instituted by Christ, Miner examines the reasons that Aquinas gives against affirming that Christ instituted the sacrament of Confirmation. Aquinas's replies to these reasons illustrate both why the Church holds that Christ instituted this sacrament, and why Confirmation is needed for salvation to be perfected in the human person. As Miner shows, Aquinas's further argumentation in the course of his question on Confirmation deepens our appreciation for this sacrament's gift of spiritual maturity/strength, following upon the spiritual rebirth of Baptism.

Bruce D. Marshall remarks upon Aquinas's statement that the sacrament of the Eucharist contains "the whole mystery of our salvation."[13] That this is so, Marshall points out, hinges upon the fact that the Eucharist, according to Aquinas, is both a sacrament and a sacrifice. In order to understand what this might mean, Marshall examines Aquinas's reasons for considering the sacrament of the Eucharist to be a "sacrifice." For Aquinas, the key is the concept of "representation." Since the Eucharist contains Christ's body and blood offered up for us, and since the power of Christ's Passion comes to us through the Eucharist, the sacramental representation of Christ's sacrifice is in fact not only a sacrament, but also a sacrifice—one and the same with Christ's sacrifice on the cross, but now represented on the altar as the Church's Eucharistic sacrifice.

The sacrament of Penance and Reconciliation is the topic of Romanus Cessario's chapter. He starts with God's graced sharing of the divine life with the human person, made in the image of God. In order to share the divine life with fallen human beings, God must have mercy upon us. Christ embodies this divine mercy from within his human life, in his supreme justice and charity on the cross. How does Christ bestow this divine mercy upon his fellow human beings? Drawing upon Aquinas's theology in light of Pope John Paul II's apostolic exhortation *Reconciliatio et paenitentia*, Cessario emphasizes the conjunction of the penitent's sorrow for sin and sacramental efficacy, through solidarity with Christ's salvific suffering. The sacrament of Reconciliation thus restores not only justice but also, and above all, the friendship with God that Christ has won for us.

---

13. *Summa Theologiae* III, q. 83, a. 4.

John F. Boyle discusses Aquinas's theology of the sacrament of the Anointing of the Sick. Boyle focuses on how Aquinas's thought on Anointing of the Sick developed over the course of his career. The question is how to distinguish this sacrament from Baptism and Reconciliation, both of which heal from sin. In his *Commentary on the Sentences of Peter Lombard*, Aquinas treats Anointing of the Sick under the analogical frame of life's movement, from entrance (Baptism) to departure (Anointing of the Sick). Given the difficulty that Anointing of the Sick is certainly not a departure from the spiritual life, Aquinas changes the analogical frame in the *Summa Contra Gentiles*. Here he treats this sacrament within the analogical frame of corporeal life, to which illness belongs. He holds that whereas both Penance and Extreme Unction are spiritual medicine, only Anointing of the Sick is spiritual and corporeal medicine. Finally, in the *Summa Theologiae*, Aquinas makes a distinction between health and robustness of health: Anointing of the Sick is ordered to attaining the latter.

Matthew Levering examines Holy Orders in Aquinas's theology. In the *Commentary on the Sentences* (found in the Supplement to the *Summa Theologiae*) Aquinas provides three objections to Holy Orders that raise the key question of how a hierarchy of office, rather than hierarchy based strictly upon wisdom or love, can accord with Christian freedom and with the mutual self-subordination to which all Christians are called. In answer, Aquinas emphasizes that unlike the hierarchy of the angels or the saints in heaven, orders in the Church on earth is not a reflection of higher grace, but rather serves instrumentally to enable human beings to participate in the grace of the Holy Spirit. This participation, as new creation, reflects the diversity that God inscribes in creation. The instrumental purpose of Holy Orders appears most fully in the Eucharist. In the *Summa Contra Gentiles*, Aquinas emphasizes that the human agents who consecrate the Eucharist *in persona Christi* must do so through a distinctive spiritual power that they receive from Christ and that they bestow upon others through the sacrament of Holy Orders.

The seventh sacrament, Marriage, is treated by Joseph W. Koterski. As with Holy Orders and Anointing of the Sick, Aquinas did not discuss Marriage in the *Summa Theologiae*, left incomplete at his death. Koterski relies instead upon the Supplement to the *Summa Theologiae* (faithfully drawn from the *Commentary on the Sentences*) and the *Summa Contra Gentiles*. He emphasizes the relationship that Aquinas develops between Marriage as an institution of natural law and Marriage as a sacrament of the New Law. This relationship relates to Aquinas's understanding of the sacraments as signs that cause in us the grace they signify. What sacred reality does the sacrament of Marriage signify, and how does the graced sacrament of Marriage build upon and elevate natural Marriage? Following Saint Paul, Aquinas holds that the sacrament of Marriage is a sign of the union of Christ and his Church in charity. As a natural institution, Marriage assists human beings in achieving the social end of our nature. The sacrament of Marriage does the same, but now in a way that takes into account both our need to be healed from the effects of the Fall, and our divinization within an indissoluble communion of persons marked by charity.

Sister Thomas Augustine Becker's chapter brings the book full circle, back to the theology of worship. Becker explores Aquinas's understanding of how we prepare our hearts and minds for receiving the grace of the Holy Spirit in the sacraments. Although God is the ultimate cause of our devotion to him, we cooperate with God interiorly by mediation and contemplation, and exteriorly by such practices as offering sacrifices and gifts, praying in consecrated places, using consecrated things in worship, employing bodily gestures that signify humility, fasting, vocally praising God in prayer and song, and *solemnitas*. After noting that Aquinas gives particular emphasis to *solemnitas*, Becker inquires more deeply into the role of *solemnitas* when the believers gather for the sacraments, professions of vows, consecrations of church buildings, and so forth. Her investigation of *solemnitas* in the rite of the Eucharist is strengthened by attention to Aquinas's account of human nature in light of Josef Pieper's understanding of "sacred language."

In short, the chapters of this book introduce the reader to the scope of Saint Thomas Aquinas's sacramental and liturgical theology. The reader gains a taste of why the Church has found Saint Thomas's thought on these subjects to be both "rigorous" and "religiously exhilarating." By means of his exploration of how each sacrament causes in us a particular configuration to Christ through the Holy Spirit, Aquinas assists believers today in understanding the role of each of the sacraments in the life of faith.

Chapter 1

The Theology of Worship: Saint Thomas

Avery Cardinal Dulles, SJ

Most of us think of Thomas Aquinas as a man totally absorbed in scholastic abstractions, a man of books who put his feelings aside in order to follow out the demands of an inexorable logic. But deeper study yields a very different picture. Trained as a boy in the Benedictine tradition, he imbibed from early youth a burning love for the liturgy. As a Dominican friar, he said Mass daily and usually attended a second Mass out of devotion. He wrote not only scholastic *summae* and learned commentaries, but hymns, prayers, and homilies, some of which we still read in the office for Corpus Christi. His systematic theology, which will be the topic of this essay, would be seriously misunderstood unless one saw behind it an author who practiced an intense and unremitting life of worship.[1]

Saint Thomas never composed a distinct treatise on worship, but he took up the theme at various points in his theological synthesis. In the *Summa Theologiae* worship is formally treated under the rubric of religion (II-II, qq. 81–100) and is discussed also in the sections on the precepts of the ceremonial law (I-II, qq. 101–8), on the priesthood of Christ (III, q. 22), and on the sacraments (III, qq. 60–90).[2]

As a systematic theologian, Thomas carefully defines his terms. Worship, he holds, is the act proper to the virtue of religion—the

---

1. David Berger, *Thomas Aquinas and the Liturgy,* 2nd ed. (Ann Arbor, MI: Sapientia Press, 2005), ch. 2.

2. Numbers in parentheses refer to the *Summa Theologiae* by part, question, and article. Where I add "ad 1" or the like, the reference is to the answer to a numbered objection proposed in the article.

virtue whereby we offer things (including ourselves) to God as signs to acknowledge his goodness and sovereignty. Because we honor God by all our virtuous actions, especially those done out of obedience to his commands, every good deed can be called religious in a broad sense of the word, but religion in the strict sense refers to acts specifically directed to the honor and glory of God (II-II, q. 81, a. 1).

On the ground that worship is a debt owed to God by reason of his excellence, Thomas takes up religion under the rubric of the cardinal virtue of justice. He recognizes, however, that religion does not fit neatly into that category, since the element of equality is missing. Although we can never give God as much honor as justice would require, we are obliged to honor him according to our capacities and the measure that God is prepared to accept (II-II, q. 81, a. 5).

Saint Thomas's theology of worship may fittingly be summarized under three main headings: the religious, the sacred, and the ecclesial.

RELIGION

The entire theological system of Saint Thomas is focused on God—God in himself, God creating and governing, and God as the goal to which all creation tends. The salvation of human beings, for Thomas, consists in union with God—a union effected through the theological virtues of faith, hope, and charity. These virtues have God as their direct object: we believe God, hope in God, and love God.

Religion is closely connected, but not identical, with the theological virtues. It presupposes that we have some measure of faith, hope, and charity, and tends to intensify these virtues. But unlike them, religion has as its direct object, not God himself, but the actions whereby we honor him. In this respect it ranks below the theological virtues (II-II, q. 81, a. 5).[3]

Saint Thomas repeatedly insists that our worship confers no benefits on God, who has all perfection eternally in himself. When we glorify God, as we do by praise, worship, and obedience, we benefit ourselves, since we draw nearer to God, in whom we find our fulfillment. Worship is theocentric because God is the one

---

3. Joseph Lécuyer, "Réflexions sur la théologie du culte selon saint Thomas," *Revue thomiste* 55 (1955): 360–1.

worshipped, and the benefit we derive from it consists in union with him (II-II, q. 81, a. 7).

Worship in the strict sense of the word (*latria*, adoration) is reserved to God alone. Following Saint John Damascene, Thomas holds that images of Christ may be adored, provided that they are regarded not as objects in their own right but purely as representations. The mind's movement toward the image as such, he explains, is the same as its movement toward the reality represented. The prohibition of images in the Old Testament, according to Thomas, was proper because the Incarnation had not yet occurred. It is impossible to make an image of God in his divine nature (III, q. 25, a. 3, ad 1; cf. II-II, q. 81, a. 3, ad 3).

Thomas concedes that veneration (*dulia*) may be given to persons and things that are closely related to God, by reason of their association, which renders them worthy of our reverence. Thus we honor saints as members of Christ, as children and friends of God, and as intercessors with God on our behalf (III, q. 25, a. 6).

Acknowledging the eminence of Mary above all other human creatures, Thomas holds that she may be venerated with a superior kind of reverence, which he calls *hyperdulia* (III, q. 25, a. 5). Relics of the saints and images of holy persons deserve *dulia* insofar as they remind us of God and direct our attention to him (III, q. 25, a. 6).

Devotion, which may be considered the heart of religion, is an interior act consisting in the ready willingness to give oneself to the service of God (II-II, q. 82, a. 1). By meditation and contemplation we can arouse in ourselves a greater love for God, the most lovable of all beings (II-II, q. 83, a. 3).

Devotion and contemplation flow over into petitionary prayer, one of the central exercises of religion. In prayer we subject ourselves to God and acknowledge him as the source of our blessings (II-II, q. 83, a. 3). Like adoration, prayer is directed to God alone, the giver of all grace and glory, but in a qualified sense we may be said to pray to angels and saints when we ask them to intercede for us by their prayers (II-II, q. 83, a. 4).

Prayer has a number of elements: the address, by which we elevate our minds to God, the petition itself, the expostulation (*ratio impetrandi*), whereby we give reasons for expecting God's help, and the thanksgiving, whereby we express our gratitude for past favors (II-II, q. 83, a. 17).

The efficacy of prayer, for Thomas, does not consist in giving God new knowledge or inducing him to change his intentions. Rather, it consists in creating conditions under which God can appropriately give gifts that he eternally wills to give, provided that the necessary conditions have been met. The change brought about by prayer is not a change in God but in the created world (II-II, q. 83, a. 2).

We should pray not only for ourselves, but also for others, since we are bound to love them, even though they be enemies (II-II, q. 83, aa. 7–8). The love of charity requires us to intercede for others. Saint Thomas compares our prayers and sacrifices for sinners to the action of one person paying off the debts of another.[4]

Saint Thomas terminates his treatise of religion by a consideration of the vices opposed to right worship. Some persons err by way of excess—not in the sense that they give too much honor to God but in the sense that their reverence is misdirected. Superstition is distorted worship; it violates the norms that make it pleasing to God and beneficial to devotion. In idolatry, we offer to creatures the adoration that is due to God alone. In divination and magic we arrogate to ourselves powers that are proper to God (II-II, qq. 92–96).

It is also possible to offend against the virtue of religion by falling short. We may err by irreverence in failing to honor holy persons and things or by sacrilege in desecrating what is sacred. These sins are offenses against God, the source of all holiness (II-II, qq. 97–100).

THE SACRED

A key element in worship is the sentiment of reverence, a kind of awe that is experienced in the presence of the holy. According to Thomas Aquinas, reverence is owed in an eminent way to God because of his surpassing excellence and power (II-II, q. 81, a. 4). It is, or can be, an expression of the infused gift of fear (II-II, q. 81, a. 2, ad 1). Such reverential fear is induced and expressed by sacred signs, which regularly accompany worship.

---

4. Ibid., 353, with references to Thomas Aquinas, *Summa Contra Gentiles*, Bk. III, ch. 158, and various texts in the *Commentary on the Sentences*.

The sacred (*sacrum*) is not quite the same as the holy (*sanctum*). Holiness usually designates an intrinsic quality that inheres in a person, notably a saint, who participates by grace in God's own life. The sacred is not an inherent but a relational reality: it belongs to whatever is connected with the divine. The prototype of the sacred is the hypostatic union—the relationship of union between the humanity of Christ and the divine Word who became incarnate in it. It is not the same as Christ's holiness, which consists in the grace that was bestowed upon him in his humanity.[5]

Cultic sacredness, which is pertinent to worship, belongs to the order of signs. Instruments of worship must point to the divine, but need not be intrinsically divinized. Saint Thomas draws an analogy from the ceremonies in royal courts. Just as kings and princes are surrounded by a certain splendor that expresses their human majesty, so the worship of God is suitably conducted at special times and places. To induce respect and submission to the divine, we need distinctively religious rites (I-II, q. 102, a. 4).

Saint Thomas recognizes three cultic realizations of the sacred: sacrifice, sacrament, and consecration.[6] Of these, the most fundamental is sacrifice, which is the source of the other two. To sacrifice, according to the etymology of the word (*sacrum facere*), is to do something to an object that is offered to God out of reverence (II-II, q. 85, a. 3). Sacrifice has two dimensions, interior and exterior. The interior dimension, which is primary, consists in acts of religion such as adoration, devotion, and prayer, by which we offer ourselves to God. The exterior dimension, which is a sign of the interior, consists in withdrawing some external object or victim from ordinary profane usage and dedicating it to God (ibid.).

In a general way, sacrifice is demanded by the natural law, but the particular modes of sacrifice practiced in a given community depend on the prescriptions of an authority, either human or divine. Different peoples accordingly have different forms of sacrifice (II-II, q. 85, a. 1). The sacrifices of the Old Law, besides fulfilling the prescriptions of natural religion, had supernatural value because they prefigured the sacrifice of Christ, in which their typology is fulfilled

---

5. See I. Mennessier, "L'Idée du "Sacré et le culte d'après saint Thomas," *Revue des sciences philosophiques et théologiques* 19 (1930): 63–82, esp. 73.

6. Ibid., 74.

(I-II, q. 103, a. 2). On the basis of the Old Testament, Saint Thomas distinguishes various kinds of sacrifice, which are needed respectively for the remission of sins, reconciliation with God, and perfect union with him (III, q. 22, a. 2). The suffering and death of a victim are not essential to the notion of sacrifice, but are fitting for sin-offerings, which are by nature satisfactory (III, q. 48, a. 2). In his sufferings and death, Christ offered a true sacrifice that acknowledged both God's majesty and the need of reparation. By lovingly offering himself, the victim of inestimable value, he superabundantly satisfied for the sins of the whole world and won graces that far exceeded what had been lost through sin. The love of Christ was the principal element in his sacrifice (III, q. 48, aa. 3–4).

Sacraments—the second form of the sacred—are sacred signs instituted for the sake of human sanctification (III, q. 61, aa. 1–2). The sacraments of the Old Law did not contain or impart grace, but they signified the grace that was to be given in the sacrifice of Christ. They were effective as attestations of justifying faith (III, q. 62, a. 6).

In the sacraments of the New Law, the power of Christ's sacrifice is applied to those who receive them (III, q. 62, a. 5). These sacraments are said to contain and confer the grace they signify. While Christ is present substantially in the Eucharist, his presence in the other sacraments is dynamic and transient, somewhat as the power of a principal cause is present in the instrument (III, q. 65, a. 3). Christ, as the principal minister, works in and through the sacraments. Since the sacraments are sacred signs, it is essential that they carry a meaning. This meaning is conveyed to some degree by the material elements and gestures, but more clearly by the accompanying words (III, q. 60, a. 6).

For a sacrament to be effective, it is necessary for the minister to posit the sacramental sign with the intention of doing what the Church does (III, q. 64, a. 9). The sacramental effect depends not on the faith or virtue of the minister, but on the power of Christ, who has covenanted himself to give his grace when the rite is properly performed (III, q. 64, a. 1). The primacy of Christ's role in the sacraments is the true meaning of the frequently misunderstood term, *ex opere operato*. Saint Thomas in the *Summa Theologiae* avoids that confusing term and speaks rather of efficacy *ex actione Christi* or *ex virtute Christi.*[7]

The fruitfulness of sacraments depends on the faith and devotion of the recipients, in the sense that their good dispositions permit the sacraments to achieve their effect. The power of Christ is operative in us through faith, whereby we unite ourselves with his Passion. "And therefore," adds Saint Thomas, "the power of the sacraments, which is directed to the removal of sin, derives chiefly from the passion of Christ" (III, q. 62, a. 5, ad 2).

The Eucharist is the sacrament par excellence, for in it "the entire mystery of our redemption is contained" (III, q. 83, a. 4). It is a sacramental sacrifice because it recalls the sacrifice of Christ, who is really present in it by means of the sacramental sign (III, q. 73, a. 5; q. 75, a. 1; q. 79, a. 5). Saint Thomas speaks of it as the "sacrament of the Last Supper," left by Christ to the Church "as a perpetual memorial of his Passion." Insofar as it is a sacrament, the Eucharist calls for participation and reception, including Holy Communion. By eating and drinking the Body and Blood of Christ, we are strengthened in charity, devotion, and reverence. "By the power of this sacrament, the soul is spiritually fed because it is delighted and in a sense inebriated with the sweetness of God's goodness" (III, q. 79, a. 1). Communion under both kinds is necessary for the integrity of the sacrament. The priest at least must receive the Precious Blood as well as the Host, and he does so in the name of the whole congregation. For this reason the sacrament is not impaired if the people receive it only under one kind (III, q. 80, a. 12).

The third cultic realization of the sacred consists in consecrations, which express the religious purposes for which certain persons or objects are reserved. Although the sacraments can validly be celebrated with minimum formalities, it is fitting, says Saint Thomas, that sacramental worship be conducted in a sacred place, with sacred vessels, and by ministers who are specially set apart for functions of worship (III, q. 83, a. 3).

---

7. This point is made by Godfrey Dieckmann in "Some Observations on the Teaching of Trent Concerning Baptism," *One Baptism for the Remission of Sins: Lutherans and Catholics in Dialogue 2*, eds. Paul C. Empie and William W. Baum (Washington, DC: National Catholic Welfare Conference, 1966), 61–70, at 67.

Persons, as well as things, can be consecrated. Certain sacraments confer on their recipients a kind of interior consecration, technically called a "character," which I shall discuss at a later point. Consecration of a person occurs also when the Church receives the religious vows by which someone undertakes to observe the evangelical counsels of poverty, chastity, and obedience. The Church officially authenticates such acts of self-donation with solemn ceremonies, so that the vowed religious has a special status in the Church (II-II, q. 184, aa. 2 and 5).[8]

In his esteem for the sacred, including consecrations, Saint Thomas manifests the sacral dimension of Catholicism, which was especially prominent in the Middle Ages. But he avoids extreme sacralism because he understands consecration not as an ontological reality inherent in the thing consecrated, but as a symbolic act conferring a new relationship and calling for a reservation of the consecrated reality to worship. Its primary function is to make people conscious of the inviolability of their religious obligations.[9]

THE ECCLESIAL DIMENSION

Thomas Aquinas wrote no treatise on the Church, but ecclesial consciousness pervades all that he wrote. In the words of a modern interpreter:

> The external and sensible aspect of consecrations is linked to the social aspect of worship and of the worshiping community. The Christian Church herself, constituted about the Eucharist by the various consecrations of its ministers and faithful, stands in the world as a sacred society, distinct and permanent in a significative way, so as to appear to all creation as a testimony to the sovereignty of God and to God's right to be worshiped.[10]

For Thomas, therefore, divine revelation is entrusted primarily to the Church, which responds in faith and gives testimony to the truth.

---

8. I. Mennessier, "Les réalités sacrées dans le culte chrétien d'après saint Thomas," *Revue des sciences philosophiques et théologiques* 20 (1931): 276–86, 453–71, at 463.

9. See Mennessier, "L'Idée du sacré," 81.

10. Mennessier, "Les réalités sacrées," 470. Translation by the author.

True worship, accordingly, is offered by the Church herself, and by individuals only within the Church, as the action of her members.

Saint Thomas is convinced that the Church is not an amorphous mass but a socially organized body—and this by the will and institution of Christ her founder. From this it follows that there are different orders and offices in the Church, with distinctive gifts and powers. The basic structure of the Church is given through the three sacraments that impart what Thomas designates in traditional terms as a "character." Baptism, Confirmation, and Holy Orders confer an indelible configuration to Christ the priest and hence an abiding capacity for engaging in actions pertaining to the public worship of the Church (III, q. 63, aa. 2–6). These sacraments can never be repeated. The sacramental character is a vehicle of the graces required for baptized, confirmed, and ordained members of the Church to perform their respective roles in Christian worship.[11]

Baptism, as the basic sacrament of regeneration and incorporation, confers a share in the common or general priesthood of all the faithful and is the "door," so to speak, to the other sacraments. By virtue of this common priesthood, lay Christians may participate in the offering of Holy Mass by a duly ordained priest, who acts in the person of Christ, and are made capable of receiving Holy Communion and other sacraments (III, q. 63, a. 6).

Confirmation gives a further degree of participation, completing and perfecting what was begun in Baptism. The confirmed receive the Holy Spirit to fortify them and are specially sealed to bear public witness to their faith (*quasi ex officio*, III, q. 72, a. 5, ad 2).

Priestly ordination gives the power to preside at the Eucharist, the supreme sacrament, and say the words of consecration in which the sacrifice is accomplished and the real presence is brought about (III, q. 82, a. 1). Priesthood includes the power to dispose the faithful to receive the sacrament, as is done in sacramental absolution from sins (Suppl. q. 8, a. 1). The priest's ministerial power over the Mystical Body flows from his power over the Eucharistic Body of Christ.

---

11. In the next few paragraphs I condense some material from my article, "The Church according to Saint Thomas," ch. 10 of *A Church to Believe In* (New York: Crossroad, 1982), 149–69, esp. 158–61.

The special designation of Bishops to their higher functions, Saint Thomas believes, is a consecration, not a sacrament, and does not confer a character (II-II, q. 183, a. 3, ad 3).[12] The Bishop, according to Saint Thomas, has the same power over the Eucharist that simple priests do, but he has larger powers with respect to the Mystical Body. He is a successor of the apostles, a prince within the ecclesiastical order, and the head of the particular church to which he has been assigned.

The chief office of the Bishop, that of teaching, is a commission to transmit and defend the faith that has been entrusted to the Church (III, q. 64, a. 2, ad 3). Bishops also administer sacraments that confer a special mission, such as Confirmation and Ordination (III, q. 65, a. 3, ad 2).

Liturgical worship, for Saint Thomas, is based on the foundational activity of Christ, who gave the Church her sacraments and ministerial office (I-II, q. 108, a. 2).[13] The sacraments may be considered from either of two perspectives. From the point of view of the divine activity, they are means of grace, but from the point of view of the human response, they are means of worship, which is directed to God by the assembly.

While the essential features of the sacramental signs are determined by divine institution, the Lord left it for the pastoral leadership of the Church, under the guidance of the Holy Spirit, to determine by human law the ceremonies surrounding the ministry of the sacraments (ibid., ad 2; cf. III, q. 64, a. 2, ad 1 and ad 3).[14]

Saint Thomas discusses these ecclesiastical rites in many different contexts. In his discussion of Baptism, he takes up the various anointings and prayers with which the Church has surrounded the essential rite. These, he says, are not required for validity, but are rightly

---

12. This is one of the few theses of Saint Thomas that was contradicted by Vatican II. *Lumen Gentium*, § 21, declares: "This synod teaches that the fullness of the sacrament of order is conferred by episcopal consecration."

13. Saint Thomas does not trace the institution of all the sacraments to Christ in his earthly ministry. Of Confirmation, for example, he says, "Christ instituted this sacrament non exhibendo sed promittendo, as is said in John 16[:7]: 'Unless I go away, the Paraclete will not come to you, but if I do I will send him to you,'" III, q. 72, a. 1, ad 1.

14. See Liam G. Walsh, "Liturgy in the Theology of St. Thomas," *The Thomist* 38 (1974): 557–83, esp. 576–7.

prescribed because they are conducive to devotion, to reverence toward the sacrament, and to the instruction of the faithful (III, q. 66, a. 10).

The sacramental liturgy of the Church, in which ministers and faithful participate according to their distinctive positions in the Church, is for Saint Thomas the heart of Christian worship. Because of his extensive treatment of the sacraments, he might appear to neglect the importance of the word. Yet he does advert to the importance of the spoken word as pertaining to the form of the sacraments themselves (III, q. 60, a. 6). In addition, he speaks about preaching in his treatise on faith. Preachers, he says, not only propose the content to be believed but by their testimony serve as "inducing causes of faith" (II-II, q. 6, a. 1). Those who have the charge of heralding the word of God are frequently assisted by a special charism, the grace of speech (*gratia sermonis*), so that their tongues become instruments of the Holy Spirit (II-II, q. 177, aa. 1–2). As a preacher and a member of the Order of Preachers, he was not unaware of the importance of proclamation, both within and outside of the liturgy.

The word of God requires a response of faith and obedience. Having believed, says Saint Thomas, we should ponder the word of God as Mary did; we should be eager to transmit God's word to others and make it fruitful in action. All of these points are concisely developed in Thomas's commentary on the Apostles' Creed.[15]

Saint Thomas does not neglect the role of oral praise and singing in the liturgy. Such vocal responses, he contends, do nothing for God but they arouse the affections of the congregation (II-II, q. 91, a. 1). Music, he adds, has special power to move the soul to delight in the things of God, provided that it is sung or played out of devotion and not merely to arouse pleasure (II-II, q. 91, a. 2). For similar reasons, Thomas approves of gestures such as kneeling and bowing, and recommends the use of painting and sculpture as aids to worship (II-II, q. 103, a. 1).

The ceremonial elements in worship, however, should not obscure the essential. Worship, like every human activity, should be directed to the glory of God, which Thomas defines as "clear knowledge accompanied by praise" (*clara cum laude notitia*, I-II, q. 2, a. 3; II-II, q. 103, a. 1, ad 3, etc.). For God to be glorified, he maintains,

---

15. Nicholas Ayo, ed., *The Sermon-Conferences of St. Thomas Aquinas on the Apostles' Creed* (Notre Dame, IN: University of Notre Dame Press, 1988), 51–3.

it is essential that the rites of religion convey the truth about God. Only in this way can worship here on earth be a fitting preparation for the heavenly liturgy in which the regime of images and sacraments will yield to the vision in which we shall see, love, and praise God without need of words or representations.[16]

In the world of our day, the ecclesial premises of Saint Thomas's theology of worship—the divinely given deposit of faith, sacraments, and apostolic ministry—are widely contested, at least outside the Catholic and Orthodox churches. Modern historicism and individualism favor a free-church approach in which the believers can reconstruct the forms of ecclesiastical government and worship and depute ministers to speak and act for them. But the Catholic Church in its official doctrine continues to insist, as Saint Thomas did, on the special sacredness of the liturgy as the work of God.

Conclusion

The great merit of Saint Thomas is to have constructed a fully systematic theology of worship, with clear definitions and distinctions, all situated within a worldview in which everything proceeds from God and finds its fulfillment in a return to God. While he makes room for the subjective element, including sentiments and emotions, Thomas's theology of worship is predominantly objective. It depends in the end upon the reality and the initiative of God. This allows for necessary adaptations to different needs and situations, but he emphasizes the necessary and universal characteristics of Christian worship.

In some minor respects, Saint Thomas's doctrine of worship is limited by the situation of the high Middle Ages in the West. For example, he overemphasizes the role of the priest without involving the congregation as much as the Second Vatican Council would have desired. He justifies the endlessly repeated Signs of the Cross in the Roman Missal of his day, the silent canon, and the reservation of the chalice to the priest-celebrant. These deficiencies can easily be remedied without detriment to the Thomistic system as a whole.

---

16. Ibid., 153.

The centerpiece of Saint Thomas's theology of worship is unquestionably the Eucharist as sacrifice and as sacrament, uniting the faithful to the Lord and to one another in him. Thomas's high theology of the Eucharist, expressed not only in his systematic works, but in his poems, hymns, and homilies, has been a source of undying inspiration to the Church for more than seven centuries and continues to resonate in the documents of Vatican II and the teaching of the most recent popes.

An assiduous study of Saint Thomas on liturgy can serve as a corrective for the unhealthy trends we have experienced in recent years, with its undue emphasis on the local community and self-expression. Saint Thomas remains a valuable resource for situating worship within a theocentric, Christological, and ecclesial framework. Only if this is done can liturgy perform its healing and sanctifying task, bringing the Christian community together in union with its divine founder and preparing it for the perfect worship of the new Jerusalem.

Chapter 2

Christ and the Metaphysics of Baptism in the *Summa Theologiae* and the *Commentary on John*

Michael Dauphinais

INTRODUCTION

The topic of this chapter fits humbly in a volume on the sacraments in Aquinas. The great controversies of our day tend to center around Marriage, Holy Orders, and the Eucharist. These are also the greatest sacraments, considered in what they signify (Marriage), or in what they are (the Eucharist), or in that to which they are ordered (Holy Orders). Aquinas himself describes Baptism as the "door of the sacraments," "since it confers on man the power to receive the other sacraments of the Church."[1] The door as a metaphor, however, delivers both negative and positive connotations to the theological student. Who wants to focus on the door when the inside of the mansion or the temple is the goal? Clearly the door is necessary to enter, but typically the door is extrinsic to the central mystery.

    Christ, however, described himself as the door or the gate. He who is the door is also the way, the truth, and the life. In this setting, Christ as the door is intrinsic to the realities inside. In what way is Baptism not extrinsic to the Christian life, but rather intrinsic? To put the question from the experience of the believing Christian,

---

1. *Summa Theologiae* III, q. 63, a. 6.

is Baptism merely an event that welcomes the individual into the Christian community, some thing that has often taken place before the individual's own intellect is sufficiently mature to remember the event? Or is Baptism an event that effects a change in the state of one's being and relationships such that it remains as an ongoing present reality? This chapter draws upon some of the integral features of Aquinas's treatment of Baptism in order to highlight the intrinsic relation of Baptism to the Christian life. To do so I will explore both Aquinas's *Summa Theologiae* and his *Commentary on John*.

Before we turn to Aquinas, it is helpful to note some recent theologians who have criticized his approach to the sacraments, since these criticisms highlight a potential misunderstanding of the use of the term *metaphysical*. In his book *Doors to the Sacred: A Historical Introduction to Sacraments in the Catholic Church*, Joseph Martos expresses the contrast as follows: "Baptism was for Aquinas a spiritual regeneration and incorporation into Christ, but it was a *hidden regeneration* occurring in the soul of the baptized infant which manifested itself only later in life, and it was a *metaphysical incorporation into Christ* which occurred through the reception of spiritual powers known collectively as the baptismal character."[2] Martos evaluates Aquinas's treatment of the regeneration and incorporation into Christ in a positive manner, but he renders a negative judgment insofar as the regeneration is "hidden" and the incorporation is "metaphysical." As Martos continues the contrast: "It was [for Aquinas] therefore also a participation in Christ's death and resurrection, as Paul had said, but it was fundamentally a *metaphysical participation* brought about by God's action on the soul."[3] Participation in the death and resurrection are again judged positively, but are then contrasted with what remains "fundamentally a metaphysical participation." In Martos's summary of the theology of Baptism, he writes, "Thus the meaning of baptism in contemporary Catholic theology is still salvation, but the meaning of salvation is becoming more experiential and less metaphysical."[4]

---

2. Joseph Martos, *Doors to the Sacred: A Historical Introduction to Sacraments in the Catholic Church* (Chicago: Triumph Books, 1991), 164–5, emphasis added.

3. Ibid., 165, emphasis added.

4. Ibid., 177.

In Martos's judgment, Aquinas's metaphysical presentation of the sacraments removes people from meaningful experiences of salvation. Instead, Martos offers the following description of Baptism: "At least we can say that baptism remains a door to the sacred for most Catholics because it is still a ritual through which they enter a religious society which stands for a sacred meaning of life and which opens the way to experiences of the sacred in childhood, adolescence, and adulthood."[5] In terms of the aforementioned distinction between an intrinsic and an extrinsic relation of Baptism to the Christian life, I would suggest that Martos's account sets up an extrinsic relation between the ritual of Baptism and the religious society with sacred meanings. In contrast, it is precisely Aquinas's *metaphysical* presentation of the sacraments that provides an intrinsic relation between Baptism and the Christian life. Such an intrinsic relation ultimately makes Baptism more meaningful to the individual believer since it is not merely an entrance ritual, but rather something that makes him or her a new creation.

Baptism in the *Summa Theologiae*

Aquinas offers a thorough treatment of the sacrament of Baptism in the *tertia pars* of his *Summa Theologiae*, in which part he considers "the Savior of all and the benefits bestowed by Him on the human race."[6] Within this larger project, Aquinas devotes a section to the sacraments in general. He writes, "After considering those things that concern the mystery of the incarnate Word, we must consider the sacraments of the Church which derive their efficacy from the Word incarnate Himself."[7] In these two prologues, Aquinas instructs his reader that the sacraments are the means through which Christ bestows his benefits upon the human race and brings them to their end of eternal life. The sacraments' efficacy is derived from Christ and therefore it is appropriate to present the sacraments after examining the mystery of the Incarnate Word. After questions 60 to 65 devoted to the sacraments in general, the questions on Baptism occupy questions 66 to 69. The place of Baptism within the *Summa*

---

5. Ibid., 176.
6. III, prologue.
7. III, q. 60, prologue.

Theologiae thus already says much about the theology of Baptism described by Aquinas. Baptism is part of God's plan for bringing human beings back to himself though Jesus Christ. Baptism has no efficacy or intelligibility apart from the Incarnation of the Word and the mysteries of his incarnate life.

When Aquinas turns to Baptism in the *Summa Theologiae*, he presents Baptism, along with the sacraments of Confirmation and Holy Orders, as a sacrament that imprints a character and confers sacramental grace.[8] Aquinas employs the threefold distinction between the *sacramentum tantum*, the *res et sacramentum*, and the *res tantum*. The *sacramentum tantum* is the material sign of the sacrament. In the case of Baptism, the *sacramentum tantum* is not water alone, but water applied to the washing of the body with the prescribed words, "I baptize you in the name of the Father, and of the Son, and of the Holy Spirit."[9] The *res et sacramentum* is both the reality and a sign of another reality. In Baptism it is the "baptismal character."[10] The *res tantum* is a reality and not a sign. In Baptism the *res tantum* is the interior justification of the sinner. The three are related through the *res et sacramentum*, which is the *res* (reality) signified by the *sacramentum tantum*, while also being simultaneously the sacramental sign of the *res tantum*: thus, it is both a reality and a sign. Aquinas relates these in Baptism as follows: "the baptismal character . . . is the *res* signified by the exterior washing and is the sacramental sign of the interior justification."[11]

This distinction between the exterior and interior components of Baptism is significant to the original question of this essay. The exterior components of Baptism have to do with all of the externals associated with Baptism: the water, the minister, the baptismal font if possible. These can be described as having an extrinsic relationship to the Christian life. They signify an interior reality and yet are not that reality. The interior components of Baptism define who and what the baptized is. Drawing upon Saint John Damascene, Aquinas views the interior components as character and justification. When considered in terms of the realities of character and justification,

---

8. III, q. 66, a. 1.

9. III, q. 66, aa. 1, 5.

10. III, q. 66, a. 1.

11. Ibid.

Baptism has an intrinsic relation to the Christian life since, apart
from these realities, there is no Christian life. Aquinas states simply
that the *sacramentum tantum* is transient; only the *res et sacramentum*
and the *res tantum* remain.[12] These realities provide the intrinsic
connection between Baptism as the door to the sacraments and the
Christian life.

The realities are not hidden. Instead, as metaphysical realities,
they exist and confer powers upon the soul possessing them. Again
drawing upon Saint John Damascene, a representative of the Eastern
tradition of theology, Aquinas identifies two facets of this interior
reality of character and justification: regeneration and illumination.

> [Damascene] sets down two things as pertaining to the ultimate reality of
> the sacrament—namely, *regeneration* which refers to the fact that man by
> being baptized begins the new life of righteousness (*iustitia*) [or justice/
> justification]; and *enlightenment* (*illuminationem*), which refers especially to
> faith, by which a man receives spiritual life.[13]

The twin themes of regeneration and illumination will characterize
Aquinas's treatment of Baptism in his *Commentary on John*.

In the treatment of the sacraments in general, Aquinas observes
that the principal effect of the sacraments is grace, the secondary
effect is character.[14] Baptism, he writes succinctly, "produces a twofold
effect in the soul, viz. the character and grace."[15] Since readers are
more familiar with the language of sacramental grace and interior
justification than that of sacramental character, let us first look at grace
and then turn to character in our examination of Baptism. In treating
the sacraments in general, Aquinas summarizes grace in general,
"As stated in I-II, q. 110, aa. 3, 4, grace, considered in itself, perfects
the essence of the soul, in so far as it is a certain participated likeness
of the Divine Nature."[16] Sacramental grace specifies this general
account of grace as participation in the divine because the sacraments derive their power from the power of the Godhead united to
the human nature of Christ in the Incarnate Word displayed most

---

12. Ibid., ad 1.
13. Ibid.
14. III, q. 62, prologue.
15. III, q. 68, a. 8.
16. III, q. 62, a. 2.

specifically in the Passion. Within the general participation in the divine nature, sacramental grace consists more specifically in the forgiveness of sins and restoration of right worship. Aquinas writes,

> Sacramental grace seems to be ordained principally to two things: namely, to take away the defects consequent on past sins, in so far as they are transitory in act, but endure in guilt; and, further, to perfect the soul in things pertaining to Divine Worship in regard to the Christian Religion.[17]

The sacramental grace describes the aforementioned interior justification effected by Baptism.

Yet what is the significance of the sacramental character and what is its relationship to Baptism? We have already seen that it is the *res et sacramentum* of Baptism and thus we know that it is signified by the external washing and also signifies the internal justification. Although the language of "character" in this context may sound odd or antiquated to contemporary readers, the reality described is not. Our contemporary society is quite familiar with the process of legal adoption that changes the child's name, rights, and duties. Such a legal adoption creates a relationship that typically does not remain extrinsic to the individual. Instead, adoption intrinsically alters the individual to be a member of the family both in perception and reality. Only the genetic lines remain distinct. One could say that the character of the family has been imprinted on the child. The language of "sacramental character" describes something akin to the "being adopted" of the child. Character in this usage provides the basic identity of the Christian.

Thus, the reader should be attentive when Aquinas states in a straightforward manner that "the eternal character is Christ himself."[18] Baptism identifies the Christian as Christ and bestows upon the Christian the mission of Christ. Drawing upon the metaphor from the Roman military of the military character or seal deputizing individuals toward a collective purpose, Aquinas argues that the sacramental character deputes the recipient for a particular end:

> Now the faithful are deputed to a twofold end; first and principally to the enjoyment of glory. And for this purpose they are marked with the seal of

---

17. III, q. 62, a. 3.
18. III, q. 63, a. 3, *sed contra.*

grace according to Ezech. [Ezekiel] 9:4: "Mark thou upon the foreheads of the men that sigh and mourn;" and Apoc. [Revelation] 7:3: "Hurt not the earth, nor the sea, nor the trees, till we sign the servants of God in their foreheads." Secondly, each of the faithful is deputed to receive, or to bestow on others, things pertaining to the worship of God. And this, properly speaking, is the purpose of the sacramental character.[19]

To summarize here, the sacramental character deputes the baptized to enjoy divine glory through the sacramental worship of God. Aquinas then continues, "Now the whole rite of the Christian religion is derived from Christ's priesthood. Consequently, it is clear that the sacramental character is essentially the character of Christ, to Whose character the faithful are likened by reason of the sacramental characters, which are nothing else than certain participations of Christ's Priesthood, flowing from Christ himself."[20] Christ's priesthood flows from Christ into those who are made like unto him by receiving his very character. Christ's character is his priesthood. The sacramental character as used by Aquinas conforms to Saint Paul's usage of the term "in Christ." The sacramental character is shorthand for Christ, his priesthood, and his Passion. When Aquinas treats the baptism of Christ, he states that "Christ is the first principle of baptism's spiritual effect."[21] Christ, thus, is both the first principle of the effect and the effect itself in the Christic character imprinted on the baptized.

Some contemporary Catholic theology, as expressed earlier by Martos, sees in the language of grace and character a tendency to isolate the believer and God; that is, a failure to discern the communal aspect of Baptism. Does Aquinas present an individualistic approach to sanctification and Baptism? In explaining why Baptism is proper to the priestly office, and not reserved only to the Bishop's office, Saint Thomas says that, "by Baptism a man becomes a participator in ecclesiastical unity, wherefore also he receives the right to approach our Lord's Table."[22] In other words, Baptism leads to ecclesiastical unity. To put another criticism in the spirit of some contemporary sacramental theologians such as Louis-Marie Chauvet,

---

19. III, q. 63, a. 3.
20. Ibid.
21. III, q. 39, a. 1, ad 3.
22. III, q. 67, a. 2.

in his *Symbol and Sacrament*, does the Aristotelian attention to the individual kinds of things as instantiations of natures with the corresponding life, powers, and activities make it difficult for Aquinas to grasp the properly communal character of the sacraments? In fact the converse is true. The attention to the relationship among natures, powers, and activities renders more sharply the communal character of the Christian life. Simply put, the Christian life requires the spiritual nature to be present in the individual. Yet the spiritual nature only has one cause; namely, Christ's Incarnation and Passion. The only way, therefore, to begin the Christian life is by real incorporation into Christ. To be united to the Head is to be united commonly with other members. No individual qua individual remains, but only the individual qua member of the Body of Christ.

The following long quote amply illustrates Aquinas's understanding of the communal aspect of Baptism:

> By baptism man is born again unto the spiritual life, which is proper to the faithful of Christ, as the Apostle says (Gal 2:20): "and that I live now in the flesh; I live in the faith of the Son of God." Now life is only in those members that are united to the head, from which they derive sense and movement. And therefore it follows of necessity that by Baptism man is incorporated in Christ as one of His members.—Again, just as the members derive sense and movement from the material head, so from their spiritual Head, i.e., Christ, do His members derive spiritual sense consisting in the knowledge of truth, and spiritual movement which results from the instinct of grace. Hence it is written (Jn 1:14, 16): "We have seen Him . . . full of grace and truth; and of His fullness we all have received." And it follows from this that the baptized are enlightened by Christ as to the knowledge of truth, and made fruitful by Him with the fruitfulness of good works by the infusion of grace.[23]

Life, sense, and movement for the Christian have no standing apart from the union with Christ. This quote supports the earlier assertion that the baptized individual is no longer an individual per se, but now is a member of Christ. The powers and activities of the baptized correspond to the spiritual nature effected by Baptism, a spiritual nature dependent upon the headship of Christ. Baptism effects this union with the head and members. The Aristotelian

---

23. III, q. 69, a. 5.

attention to individual substances does not create an individualism. Instead, the attention to kinds highlights the difference brought about by Baptism and the social and communal relationships now established.

Aquinas summarizes the effect of Baptism as spiritual regeneration: "The essential effect of Baptism is that for which Baptism was instituted, namely, the begetting of men unto spiritual life."[24] Aquinas frequently employs the parallel with natural generation, and here he does so in defense of the ecclesial practice of the Baptism of infants. As he puts it,

> The spiritual regeneration effected by Baptism is somewhat like carnal birth [*nativitati carnali*], in this respect, that as the child while in the mother's womb receives nourishment not independently, but through the nourishment of its mother, so also children before the use of reason, being as it were in the womb of their mother the Church, receive salvation not by their own act, but by the act of the Church.[25]

The language of the Church as mother shows the fundamental interconnectedness of the baptized as members of Christ's body.

The distinction between sacramental grace and sacramental character also allows us to understand the effects of post-baptismal sin. Grace is the ultimate, or final, effect of Baptism (*ultimus effectus sacramenti*) and as such requires right faith on the part of the recipient of the sacrament; the imprinting of the character is the proximate effect effected directly by the power of God (*per virtutem Dei*), and as such does not require right faith on the part of the recipient (cf. *Summa Theologiae* III, q. 68, a. 8). The fact that right faith is not necessary demonstrates the reality that the human being cannot in any way contribute to the original imprinting of Christ and his priesthood on the soul. Conditional upon the participation in the priesthood of Christ, the individual as a member of Christ can now cooperate with the offer of grace. This also means that the Baptism cannot be repeated since the baptized person does not have the ability to remove the Christic character. Even with mortal sin and the rejection of the theological virtue of faith, the baptized member of the Church retains the character while losing the grace. Since the character is ordered to the grace, the character is useless for the person until

---

24. III, q. 69, a. 8.
25. III, q. 68, a. 9, ad 1.

the person returns with faith, repents for sins, and receives the sacrament of Penance.

The foregoing overview of Baptism is sufficient to display the intrinsic relation of Baptism to the Christian life. In other words, Baptism effects the participation of the faithful in the priesthood of Christ and the justification he imparts. From this perspective, recognition of the continual implications of one's Baptism is necessary to live the Christian life.

BAPTISM IN AQUINAS'S *COMMENTARY ON THE GOSPEL OF JOHN*

Let us now turn to the reality of Baptism as displayed in the encounter of Nicodemus with Jesus, described by Aquinas in his *Commentary on the Gospel of John*. The central image is *regeneratio spiritualis*, a theme already central to the treatment of Baptism in the *Summa Theologiae*.

Nicodemus's encounter with Jesus in the third chapter of John is marked by its memorable dialogue. Nicodemus comes at night and initially declares his recognition of Jesus as a man from God who has performed great signs. Aquinas focuses on Jesus' two initial responses to Nicodemus. First, "Amen, amen, I say to you, unless one is born again, he cannot see the kingdom of God" (John 3:3). Second, "Amen, amen, I say to you, unless one is born again of water and the Holy Spirit, he cannot enter the kingdom of God. What is born of flesh is itself flesh; and what is born of Spirit is itself spirit" (John 3:5–6). Aquinas is aware that the language of "born again" is more properly rendered "born from above," but the Latin of the Vulgate allows for both interpretations as does the Greek of the New Testament.

First, "unless one is born again, he cannot *see* the kingdom of God" (emphasis added). Aquinas here draws on the metaphor of sight for knowledge. To see the kingdom of God corresponds not to material vision, but describes an intellectual grasp of the mysteries of God, specifically in the Incarnate Word. Aquinas analyzes the scene, observing that Jesus handles Nicodemus's initial inquiry in an effective manner: Jesus neither affirms nor denies Nicodemus's statements, but instead redirects Nicodemus's attention to the principle of his statements. Recall that Nicodemus first approaches Jesus and says that Jesus is "from God" and "has God with him" because of the works he has done. Nicodemus thus can be said to view Jesus as a wise teacher and rabbi and perhaps a divine prophet. Jesus seeks to elevate Nicodemus's understanding of himself and the kingdom. Aquinas's approach here fits within his overall approach to the Gospel account of John as specifically dealing with "things pertaining to the divinity of Christ" (§ 430; cf. prologue). To know the truth about Jesus' divinity requires spiritual knowledge. Or, in the original words, to see the kingdom of God requires to be born again or from above. Aquinas glosses Jesus' first response to Nicodemus, "As if to say: It is not strange that you regard me as a mere man, because one cannot know these secrets of the divinity unless he has achieved a spiritual regeneration" (§ 431). It is not only the case that the Incarnate Word causes spiritual regeneration; spiritual regeneration causes the recognition of Jesus as the Incarnate Word.

Aquinas employs Aristotelian concepts to indicate the profundity of the language of "seeing" the kingdom of God. He comments that "since vision is an act of life, then according to the diverse kinds of life there will be diversity of vision" (§ 432). There is the natural intellectual vision that corresponds to our natural life; so also there is a spiritual vision corresponding to spiritual life. Aquinas describes the spiritual life as that "by which man is made like to God and other holy spirits" (§ 432). To see the kingdom of God, thus, is a circumlocution for divinization. Only those who are like God can see God. Drawing further upon the image of an earthly kingdom, Aquinas expands the term "kingdom of God" here to include the glory and dignity, or royal majesty, of God. God's glory and dignity is manifested most specifically in "the mysteries of eternal salvation which are seen through the justice of faith" (§ 432). The language of the kingdom of God, in Aquinas's exegesis, thus includes both the believer's participation in the divine nature and the mysteries of salvation including chiefly the Incarnation and the Passion.

To support the metaphysical argument about kinds of life and kinds of sight, Aquinas presents a list of biblical quotations (§ 432). "The sensual man does not perceive those things that pertain to the Spirit of God" (1 Corinthians 2:14). "No one knows the things of God but the Spirit of God" (1 Corinthians 2:11). "You did not receive

the spirit of slavery, putting you in fear again, but the spirit of adoption" (Romans 8:15). "He saved us by the cleansing of regeneration
[*per lavacrum regenerationis*] in the Holy Spirit" (Titus 3:5). Here we
can see a recurring theme. The Aristotelian language of natures,
powers, and activities does not move away from the biblical world, but
effectively underscores the totality and reality of the Pauline description of transformation in Christ.

An aspect worth considering concerns Aquinas's correspon-
dences between body and soul and natural life and spiritual life.
Aquinas carefully delineates that the natural life includes both the
body and the soul. There is no imprecise equivalent of the soul with
the spiritual life. Moreover, the manner in which Aquinas utilizes
the distinction between the natural life and the spiritual life emphasizes the hylomorphic unity of the human being. For just as the
natural life includes the body and the soul, so does the spiritual life
include the body and the soul. The spiritual regeneration, or spiritual
rebirth, partially renews the soul in this life and will fully renew
the body and the soul in the next (§ 433). This unity of human nature
is displayed through Aquinas's treatment of the several stages of
spiritual regeneration. In the Old Law, spiritual regeneration was
"imperfect and symbolic." In the New Law, spiritual regeneration is
"evident" yet "imperfect" since "we are renewed only inwardly by grace,
but not outwardly by incorruption." In heaven, regeneration is "perfect" since "we will be renewed both inwardly and outwardly" (§ 433).

After Jesus declares the necessity of being born again or
born from above, Nicodemus responds in a manner showing further
misunderstanding, asking, "How can a man be born when he is old?
Can he enter a second time into his mother's womb and be born?"
(John 3:4). Jesus then responds, "Amen, amen, I say to you, unless
one is born again of water and the Holy Spirit, he cannot enter the
kingdom of God. What is born of flesh is itself flesh; and what is born
of Spirit is itself spirit" (John 3:5–6). Aquinas understands the
language of being born again "of water and the Spirit" as explaining
the manner in which the spiritual regeneration is to be accomplished.

It is clear that a spiritual regeneration must come from the
spirit, but why the conjunction of water? Aquinas employs this
explanation of the use of water in Christian Baptism to offer a deeper
explanation of the dimensions of the spiritual regeneration to the

Christian life. Aquinas offers three reasons for the use of water to accompany rebirth in the Spirit. First, human nature includes both material and immaterial elements. Since the whole of man is to be regenerated, the Spirit signifies the regeneration of the soul, and the water signifies the regeneration of the body (§ 443). Second, human knowledge comes through the senses. If this is the case on the level of natural knowledge to know spiritual things through sensible things, it is fitting to come to know spiritual regeneration through the sensible sign of water. Third, the sacraments have power from the Incarnate Word. Thus the water corresponds to the incarnate aspect and the Spirit corresponds to the Word.

Aquinas summarizes the centrality of spiritual regeneration in Baptism thus:

> Then when [Jesus] says, "What is born of flesh is itself flesh," he proves by reason that it is necessary to be born of water and the Holy Spirit. And the reasoning is this: No one can reach the kingdom unless he is made spiritual; but no one is made spiritual except by the Holy Spirit; therefore, no one can enter the kingdom of God unless he is born again of the Holy Spirit. (§ 447)

Being spiritual is necessarily related to the spiritual rebirth. Not only is spiritual rebirth necessarily for spiritual life, both are effected by Christ. Aquinas writes, "Now there are two causes of spiritual regeneration, namely, the mystery of the incarnation of Christ, and his passion" (§ 465). Baptism applies the fruits of the Incarnation and Passion of Christ to the baptized by making the baptized be reborn as a member of the kingdom of God inaugurated by Christ.

Conclusion

Baptism thus can be said to be intrinsically related to the Christian life. Given the parallel to natural generation, one can consider the relation between the life, power, and activity of an individual and the act of generation that began that life, power, and activity. Although temporally separated from the moment I was generated, it is clear that there was no way for me to be who and what I am apart from the act of my generation to be who and what I am. To employ the metaphor of the door and the window, there is no other window through which

I could have entered into my being. Thus, natural generation is intrinsically related to the life, power, and activities of the natural life. One can also consider the relation of the creator and creation. Creation expresses an ongoing relationship of causality in which the present existence of all things depends upon the perfect existence of *ipsum esse subsistens*. There is not a deistic creator who wound up the clock of the cosmos and then stepped back. No, participated existence depends fully and completely at each moment and every point of space on the creator. Recall that Baptism imprints a character according to Aquinas. The character is the character of Christ specifically as a participation in his priesthood. While it is true that Baptism is a singular event that cannot be repeated, it also instantiates a participation in the priesthood of Christ. Thus the ongoing participation is always intrinsically related to the sacrament of Baptism. Consider Romans 6:3–4, "Do you not know that all of us who have been baptized into Christ Jesus were baptized into his death? We were buried therefore with him by baptism into death, so that as Christ was raised from the dead by the glory of the Father, we too might walk in newness of life." The reference to the past event indicates the kind of living possible in the present.

Aquinas's metaphysical analysis of Baptism does not exclude experiential significance, as asserted in Martos's contrast between metaphysical and experiential. A proper understanding of metaphysical is neither hidden nor individualistic. Instead, a metaphysical analysis of Baptism refers to the realities of Baptism. Baptism confers of sacramental grace and character—realities that both come from and lead to the mystery of the Incarnation and Passion of Christ.

Chapter 3

Aquinas on the Sacrament of Confirmation

Robert C. Miner

In comparison to the lively controversies over Baptism, Marriage, confession, Holy Orders, and the Eucharist, discussions of Confirmation may strike the causal observer as somewhat anodyne. Yet this appearance is misleading, for the character of Confirmation as a sacrament is anything but evident. In what follows, I will set out a reading of question 72 of the *tertia pars* of the *Summa Theologiae*. The reading interrogates the grounds upon which Aquinas regards Confirmation as a sacrament and suggests the deeper connections between sacramental theology and fundamental anthropology.

In question 72 of the *tertia pars* of the *Summa Theologiae*, Thomas asks whether Confirmation is a sacrament. The question divides into three main parts.

1. Does Confirmation as sacrament exist? (Article 1—the *an sit*)
2. What is confirmation? (Articles 2–7—the *quid sit*)
   Confirmation as matter/form composite (Articles 2–4)
   Its effects (Articles 5–7)
3. The sacrament's administration (Articles 8–12)

Is confirmation a sacrament? Before considering article 1 of question 72 of the *tertia pars*, it is important to notice something about the *Summa* in general. The treatment of the last end, the passions, and the virtues and vices that constitute the *secunda pars* is a long preparation for the delayed (and therefore dramatic) entrance of Christ. To complete the "work of theology," Thomas says in the prologue of the *tertia pars*, "our consideration" must shift to Christ, the Savior of mankind. Thus the *tertia pars* of the *Summa* is devoted to a threefold consideration of the Savior himself, of his sacraments, and of the end of immortal life. Notice the language of the triad's second member. Thomas is not treating "the sacraments," but *His* sacraments. Question 60 begins (without completing) a consideration *de sacramentis eius*. From the very beginning of the *tertia pars*, Thomas uncompromisingly places the sacraments in direct relation to Christ. They are his sacraments.

With this in mind, one sees that the first article of question 72—"whether confirmation [is] a sacrament"—is at the same time a question about the relation of Confirmation to Christ. For Luther, it seemed evident that Christ did not institute the sacrament of Confirmation. In *The Babylonian Captivity of the Church* he writes:

> It is amazing that it should have entered the minds of these men to make a sacrament of confirmation out of the laying on of hands. We read that Christ touched the little children in that way, and that by it the apostles imparted the Holy Spirit, ordained presbyters, and cured the sick; as the Apostle writes to Timothy: "Do not be hasty in the laying on of hands." (1 Tim. v. 22)[1]

Luther proceeds to reduce the sacrament to an easy duty designed to justify the power of Bishops. (In considering the brutality of this reduction of Confirmation to the will to power, one is reminded that Nietzsche is not merely the son of a Lutheran pastor, but a genuine heir of Luther himself.) "We seek sacraments that have been divinely instituted," Luther declares, "and among these we see no reason for numbering confirmation."[2] Interestingly, the *videtur quod* of question 72, article 1, makes a stronger case than the *Babylonian Captivity* does for the claim that Christ did not institute the sacrament. It gives four reasons:

1. In the New Testament, we do not read of Confirmation described as a sacrament.
2. In the Old Testament, Confirmation is not prefigured as a type of the New Law, unlike Baptism and other sacraments.

---

1. Martin Luther, "The Babylonian Captivity of the Church," trans. A. T. W. Steinhäuser, F. C. Ahrens, and A. R. Wentz, in *Three Treatises* (Philadelphia: Fortress Press, 1970), 219.

2. Ibid.

3. Sacraments are directed toward the end of salvation. Because
   young children who have been baptized can be saved without Confirmation, Confirmation is unnecessary and therefore
   not a genuine sacrament.
4. The basic function of the sacraments is to conform man to Christ.
   But since we never read of Christ himself being confirmed, man
   cannot be conformed to Christ through something alien to Christ.

Given the apparent absence of direct scriptural evidence for
the view that Christ instituted Confirmation, how can it be a sacrament? Aquinas knows (and rejects) the view that Confirmation was
not instituted until the time of the councils. He reiterates that if
Confirmation is a sacrament, then Christ must be its author. But
given the apparent absence in scripture of an explicit act of divine
institution, how can this be held? Thomas makes a distinction
between two kinds of institution. One might institute something by
immediately "exhibiting" it. Alternatively, one might institute something by "promising" it, that is, "sending it forth" (*promittendo*) at
a later date. Thus Christ says in John 16:7, "If I go not, the Paraclete
will not come to you, but if I go, I will send (*mittam*) Him to you."
When Christ sends the Paraclete to the Church, he sends the "plenitude of the Holy Spirit," which did not fittingly appear until after
the Resurrection and the Ascension. To deny that Christ could
institute the sacrament in this way would be to restrict, arbitrarily and
heretically, his power to direct exhibition during his life on earth.

This establishes the possibility that Christ institutes
Confirmation. It also shows why nothing in the Old Law expressly
prefigures Confirmation. Confirmation is the "sacrament of the
fullness of grace" (q. 72, a. 1, ad 2). The fullness of grace, considered
precisely as fullness, could not correspond to anything in the Old
Law, since (as Aquinas says, quoting Hebrews) "the Law brought
nothing to perfection" (Hebrews 7:19, quoted at q. 72, a. 1, ad 2).
Perhaps more problematic is the apparent non-necessity of the sacrament. The third objector cites baptized children who die prior to
being confirmed, but still go to heaven. Does this show that the
sacrament is in no sense necessary? It does not, unless one assumes
an impoverished conception of necessity. "All sacraments are necessary for salvation in some manner" (q. 72, a. 1, ad 3). Some are
necessary for salvation simply, and others are necessary for its perfection.

This is a familiar distinction. Sexual intercourse is not necessary for a wedding to occur, but it is necessary for the wedding's consummation. This analogy is not misleading, since in article 11 Thomas explicitly describes confirmation as the *ultima consummatio* of the work begun by the sacrament of Baptism.[3] Thus Confirmation, while not simply necessary, is necessary *ad perfectionem salutis*. One can be saved without Confirmation, Thomas concludes, but he quickly adds that this holds only provided that the sacrament is not omitted *ex contemptu sacramenti*.

In the response of article 1, Aquinas argues more fully that Confirmation must be a sacrament. For any of the "special effects" of grace, he contends, there is a corresponding "special sacrament." By "special effects," Thomas has in mind not the divine counterpart of Industrial Light and Magic, but the particular changes wrought by grace in the life of the human person. One might wonder whether the capacity of grace to produce an unlimited number of effects in a person would not imply an unlimited number of sacraments. Aquinas would answer that while the effects produced by grace are materially many, they may formally be reduced to the initial regeneration of spiritual life and its subsequent perfection. Baptism corresponds to the first effect; Confirmation to the second. Since sensible and bodily things bear a likeness to spiritual and intelligible things, one may see this basic dynamic inscribed in natural beings that first receive bodily life, and then undergo bodily growth, by which they are led "to their complete age." To better discern the intelligibility of Christ's dual institution of Baptism and Confirmation, Aquinas draws upon the natural analogues of birth and growth, generation and augmentation.[4]

Attending to both scripture and the manner in which the body's life images that of the spirit, Aquinas concludes that Christ is the author of the sacrament. Further applying the principle that the sensible is an analogue of the spiritual, Thomas turns to the question "What is confirmation?" in article 2 by attending to its matter. Here

---

3. He does, however, warn against taking the metaphor too literally: "confirmationis sacramentus est *quasi* ultima consummatio" (q. 72, a. 11).

4. In his valuable treatment of the question, Benedikt Tomás Mohelník, OP, proposes that the analogy between natural generation and supernatural growth is an instance of the analogy of proportionality (*'Gratia augmenti': Contribution au débat contemporain sur la confirmation* [Fribourg: Academic Press Fribourg, 2005], 211). Whether or not this is true, one must agree with his observation that "la notion d'analogie est elle-même analogique."

he shows why chrism, the mixture of olive oil with balsam, is the *conveniens materia*, the fitting matter, of the sacrament. Making the case from both nature and scripture, Thomas gives the scriptural argument first. The plenitude of the Holy Spirit, of which Confirmation is the expression, is appropriately signified by oil, since Christ is "anointed with the oil of gladness" (q. 72, a. 2). The sign of perfection in the life of a human being is her full entrance into communal life. Oil, especially when mixed with balm, naturally signifies community, since it is fragrant and "overflows toward others" (*redundant ad alios*: q. 72, a. 2).[5] Another reason for regarding oil as the suitable matter of the sacrament is that Confirmation is related not simply to spiritual existence, but to being "on fire" with the plenitude of the Holy Spirit. As the passive power that serves as the "matter and kindling" of fire, oil signifies the capacity of Confirmation to kindle what is already present by virtue of Baptism. Thomas adds that the olive tree, "through being an evergreen (*semper frondibus virens*), signifies the refreshing (*virorem*) and merciful operation of the Holy Spirit" (q. 72, a. 2, ad 3). Finally, olive oil is *conveniens materia* because, though widely available in all parts of the world, it is not as easy to obtain as water. This is a sensible sign of the immaterial reality that Baptism is the "sacrament of absolute necessity" (q. 72, a. 2, ad 4), whereas Confirmation (as we have seen) is a sacrament of relative necessity.

Turning to the form of the sacrament in article 4 of question 72, Aquinas inquires into the fittingness of the verbal formula, "I sign you with the sign of the cross; I confirm you with the chrism of salvation; in the name of the Father and of the Son and of the Holy Spirit. Amen." The first objector argues from the Christocentric nature of the sacraments to the conclusion that the words quoted above cannot be the proper form of the sacrament. The argument is that neither Christ nor the apostles are recorded using these very words. One conventionally Catholic way of replying to this charge is to cite the final sentence of the Gospel according to John:

---

5. On the significance of the oil's odor, Saint Bonaventure adds that the fragrance of "good reputation and honest life" signifies the "sweet odor of life and reputation, lest there be some contradiction between language and conscience or between language and reputation which would cause such a profession to be rejected by man and disapproved by Christ." See *Breviloquium*, Part VI, ch. 8.

"But there are also many other things which Jesus did; were every one of them to be written, I suppose that the world itself could not contain the books that would be written" (John 21:25).[6] The reply that Thomas gives is less conventional and more interesting. Instead of citing John, he quotes Dionysius. "It is not right [*non iustum*] to bring out of hiding [*ex occulto*] the highest invocations [*consummativas invocationes*]"—that is, "the words by which the sacraments are brought to completion, whether the mystical meaning, or the powers in them worked by God. Rather, our sacred tradition teaches them without display [*sine pompa*], that is, secretly [*occulte*]" (q. 72, a. 4, ad 1).[7] To search scripture for the exact words of institution is a mistake. Rather, we should trust "our sacred tradition," which teaches that Confirmation requires the form, and seeks the rationale for the form. Thomas finds the rationale in a correspondence between the three parts of the verbal formula and the three things necessary for the sacrament's purpose, which—Aquinas tells us now—is *robur spiritualis pugnae*, "spiritual strength for battle" (q. 72, a. 4).[8]

Robur connotes the strength, solidity, and firmness of an oak tree. At this precise point in the dialectic, *robur* becomes a key term for the whole question. Prior to article 4, *robur* occurs once. Beginning with article 4, the term occurs 11 times. In each of the occurrences except for one, *robur* is accompanied by the adjective *spirituale*. To understand Confirmation, then, one must understand what Aquinas means by "spiritual strength." By the time she arrives at question 72 of the *tertia pars*, the ideal reader of Saint Thomas will have acquired an adequate idea of spiritual strength. She will have read and thoroughly assimilated the string of 18 questions on the virtue of fortitude that appears in the *secunda-secundae*. But to accommodate other readers, Aquinas provides a teaching on the nature of spiritual strength in the remainder of question 72. First, Aquinas says in article 6, the clear

---

6. See, for example, Leo J. Trese, *The Faith Explained*, 3rd ed. (Princeton: Scepter, 2001), 337.

7. Cf. Dionysius, *On the Ecclesiastical Hierarchy*, ch. 7.

8. The phrase can, of course, be rendered "strength for spiritual battle." But given the frequency of "*robur spiritualis*" with no accompanying *pugnae*, I prefer "spiritual strength for battle." (I do not deny that both the mode of strength and the battle are fundamentally spiritual in character.) Some (e.g., Tanqueray) have inferred that for Aquinas that the function of confirmation is to make a person a "soldier of Christ." Mohelník correctly observes that "cette idée n'est pas celle de St Thomas." Mohelník, '*Gratia augmenti*,' 72; see also 208–10.

sign of spiritual strength is the capacity for confessing the faith of
Christ publicly (q. 72, a. 6, ad 1). (Think of the remarkable reversal
of Victorinus, the proud translator of Platonic books, as told to
Augustine and retold in *Confessions* VIII.) Confirmation provides the
grace for a believer, no matter what her temperament or disposition,
to profess her faith publicly.

Can a person do this without having been confirmed? Yes,
Aquinas says. While divine power (*virtus divina*) fittingly flows
to human beings through the sacraments, it is not "fettered" (*alligata*)
to them. Though God typically provides spiritual strength through
the sacrament of Confirmation, he can bestow its proper effect by any
means He wishes, just as a person can receive the remission of sins
without Baptism. "Yet, just as none receive the effect of baptism without the desire of baptism, so none receive the effect of confirmation,
without the desire of confirmation" (q. 72, a. 6, ad 1). Confirmation
does not destroy, but rather perfects nature. For a person who lacks
any desire to confess the faith of Christ publicly, the presence or
absence of the sacrament makes little difference. Aquinas does not
think that the sacraments are magic. On the contrary, they work
with our present disposition, elevating to a new, supernatural level
what is already contained in our nature. (This requires, as Aquinas
observes, that Confirmation be administered only to a person in
a state of grace [q. 72, a. 7, ad 2].)

Aquinas makes this abundantly clear in article 7, asking
whether *gratia gratum faciens* is conferred by the sacrament. Though it
is not incorrect to render *gratia gratum faciens* by the familiar phrase
"sanctifying grace," something is lost if we fail to attend to the
phrase's literal meaning: "making one pleasing or acceptable [to God]."
By conferring spiritual strength, and thus elevating our nature
without violating it, God makes us acceptable to him in a radically
new way. One might wonder why this would be the case. Is not
Baptism sufficient to make us pleasing to God? Why is another sacrament required? For Luther, to suggest the necessity of Confirmation
is to doubt the efficacy of the singular grace symbolized by Baptism.[9]

---

9. Mohelník provocatively suggests that the *tertia pars*'s argument for the necessity of
Confirmation in addition to Baptism has deep roots in the Trinitarian theology presented in the
prima pars. "La lecture attentive du traité sur les sacrements dans la *Somme de théologie* laisse
apercevoir avec quelle rigueur St Thomas suit la règle non exprimée explicitement, mais pourtant

Aquinas, by contrast, holds that Baptism cleanses the soul of all original and actual sin up to the administration of the sacrament. But, he writes, "*gratia gratum faciens* is not only given for the remission of guilt (*culpa*), but also for growth (*augmentum*) and firmness (*firmitatem*) of righteousness" (q. 72, a. 7, ad 1). God intends not only to begin his good work, but to complete it. This holds particularly in the present case. A person must not only be cleansed of sin, but also become a spiritual grown-up. Thomas is very clear on this point: "though he who is confirmed may be adult in body (*adultus corporaliter*), nonetheless he is not yet spiritually adult (*adultus spiritualiter*)" (q. 72, a. 10, ad 1). To be cleansed of guilt, while remaining no more spiritually developed than after the moment of Baptism, would not be fitting for the human person whose natural development entails not only birth, but also growth and firmness.

In the same article, Aquinas makes two other crucial points. First, he deepens the scriptural context of Confirmation by comparing what happened to the apostles at Pentecost to what happens to the individual soul at the moment of the sacrament's reception. "In this sacrament the Holy Spirit is given to the baptized for strength, just as He was given to the apostles on the day of Pentecost, as is read in Acts 2, and just as He was given to the baptized through the laying of hands of the Apostles" (q. 72, a. 7). Luther professes to be surprised that anyone would make a sacrament of this laying of hands. Thomas would be surprised at the surprise. He would wonder why Luther refuses to read the Spirit's grace-conferring activity in the life of an individual as anything but a microcosmic analogue of the activity of Christ vis-à-vis the Church, and the apostles vis-à-vis the baptized. Second, Aquinas acknowledges the etymological connection between *firmitas*, stability, and the name *confirmatio*. The manner of the acknowledgment is of some interest. *Firmitas* does not merely signify the extra firmness conferred by the sacrament. More basically, it denotes the prior firmness of soul that must already be possessed in order for Confirmation to do its work. Thus the *gratia gratum faciens* conferred by Confirmation, far from violating the soul's nature, "is given to confirm what is there before (*prius*)" (q. 72, a. 7, ad 2).

---

respectée: le baptême configure le fidèle au Christ, la confirmation confère la plénitude de l'Esprit Saint." Ibid., 136.

I have emphasized the grounding of Confirmation in the naturalness of the distinction between childhood and maturity, generation, and augmentation. Since natural things are essentially a likeness of spiritual things, one can gain some understanding of spiritual things by looking at natural things. This point is basic to Thomas's typical mode of proceeding. From what is most knowable to us—the order of the sensible—we ascend to what is most knowable in itself—the order of the spiritual. However, Thomas never loses sight of the manner in which the higher not only builds upon the lower, but also transcends it. Thus in article 8, he underscores the fact that the spiritual strength provided by Confirmation does not depend on chronological or bodily age. Even in childhood, Thomas says, "man can attain to the perfection of spiritual age." He quotes from the book of Wisdom: "Venerable old age is not that of long time, nor counted by the number of years" (Wisdom 4:8). To strengthen the point, he cites the example of children martyrs who, "on account of the spiritual strength of the Holy Spirit which they had received, contended bravely for Christ *usque ad sanguinem*," literally "up to their blood." This example is a poignant reminder of why in question 72 *robur* is almost invariably accompanied by *spirituale*. The proper effect of Confirmation is *spiritual* strength. While Aquinas wants to manifest the fittingness of Confirmation by attention to the natural rhythms of birth and growth, he does not do so through any crude reduction of the spiritual to the material.

To recapitulate: *robur spirituale* involves public confession, sanctifying grace, spiritual maturation, and potential martyrdom. In a way, these things are matters of the heart, requiring courage more than intellectual development. If this is the case, then why is the sacrament administered on the forehead? Thomas raises this question in article 9. Spiritual strength is conferred for the sake of *pugna*— fight, battle, combat. (Some may find the military analogy disturbing, but Thomas does not—and nor, for that matter, does the peace-loving Franciscan Bonaventure.)[10] As a soldier receives his leader's sign on

---

10. In fact, as the treatment of the *Breviloquium* dramatically attests, Bonaventure gives proportionally more emphasis to the military analogy. Showing that the profession of faith accompanying Confirmation is not only "complete" and "clear," but also "undaunted," Bonaventure concludes:

Such a profession ought to be undaunted so that a person does not out of shame or fear refuse to tell the truth, and so that he is not in time of persecution afraid or ashamed publicly

his forehead, so a man fittingly receives on his forehead the Sign of the Cross with chrism. This further emphasizes the intrinsically public and communal character of Confirmation. As Aquinas reminds us, the forehead is the "most manifest" (*maxime manifestus*) part of the human body. If spiritual maturity requires the public manifestation and profession of the faith of Christ, then the sign of Confirmation is most appropriately received on the forehead. The motion from privately held faith to public manifestation, Thomas adds, serves to echo the apostolic transition from hiding in the upper room to public appearance, made after reception of the Holy Spirit.

In the same article, Aquinas locates a second—and perhaps more psychologically profound—reason for giving the sacrament on the forehead. Referring implicitly to the 27 questions on the passions in the *prima-secundae*, Aquinas writes:[11]

Anyone is impeded from a free confession of the name of Christ on account of two things—that is, on account of fear, and on account of shame. Now both of these things are most of all manifested on the forehead, on account of its nearness to the imagination, and because vital spirits rise directly from the heart to the forehead, whence "those who are ashamed, blush, and those who are in fear, go pale," as is said in Book IV of the *Ethics*. And thus a person is signed with chrism in the forehead,

to confess the ignominious death of Christ on the cross for fear of suffering a similar punishment and ignominious passion and such a fear and shame appear especially on the face and principally on the forehead, hence, to ward off all shamefacedness and fear, the powerful hand which confirms is there imposed and the cross is marked on the forehead so that one may not ashamed publicly to profess that death or fear to sustain any punishment or ignominy whatsoever for the profession of the name of Christ, if the occasion should so demand.

Then a person shall be, as it were, a true fighter anointed for battle; a strong soldier bearing the symbol of his King on his forehead and the triumphal standard of His cross with which he is prepared to penetrate the mighty strongholds of the enemy. One cannot be free to proclaim the glory of the cross if the punishment and ignominy of the cross is feared. Thus St. Andrew says: "If I were ashamed of the ignominy of the cross, I would not proclaim the glory of the cross."

11. Though I cannot argue the point in detail here, the necessity for Confirmation in addition to Baptism is inherently linked to the anthropology that requires a distinction between the concupiscible and irascible, made by Aquinas in question 81 of the *prima pars*, and enlarged in question 23 of the I-II. The object of the concupiscible is the basic object of desire, the pleasant good; the object of the irascible is the useful good that cannot be acquired without a fight (*pugna*). To say this another way: the prominence of *pugna* in the description of Confirmation may be connected to the role played by *pugna* in the description of the irascible's distinction from the concupiscible. For a treatment of the concupiscible/irascible distinction, see my *Thomas Aquinas on the Passions: A Study of Summa Theologiae Ia-IIae* 22–48 (Cambridge: Cambridge University Press, 2009), pp. 46–57.

so that neither on account of fear nor on account of erubescence [blushing] does he omit to confess the name of Christ (q. 72, a. 9).

If allowed to rule, the passions of fear and shame can prevent us from becoming spiritual adults. They may hinder us from engaging in spiritual combat, which has less to do with conventional images of fighting, and far more to do with publicly confessing the faith of Christ (with all that entails). Why do we so often resemble Peter and deny Christ? Why do we fail to acknowledge Christ publicly? Why are we spiritual wimps? In this article, Aquinas has isolated two primary reasons. Either we are afraid of the consequences, or else we are ashamed.

Aquinas appears to teach that Confirmation provides spiritual strength by eliminating the passions that prevent us from freely confessing the name of Christ. That fear and shame can have precisely this effect is true. But one must also remember that for Aquinas, fear, shame, and the other passions are fundamentally part of created nature. As such, they have their proper role to play in the spiritual life of the human person. What is generally true of nature—that it must be elevated in order to reach its supernatural destination—is evidently true of the passions of fear and shame. If these passions are not put in their proper place by the supernatural strength provided by grace through the sacrament of Confirmation, they will enfeeble us. Perhaps the least obvious but most profound effect of *robur spirituale* consists not in the elimination of these passions, but in their transformation, so that they aid the embodied intellect in its motion toward the end. As acts of the "lower appetite," the passions provide the rational animal with a primal energy required for complete flourishing, a kind of "strength from below." Inversely but complementarily, Confirmation provides a kind of "strength from above." Both are required to move the rational creature forward in its quest for eternal beatitude, the practical purpose of *sacra doctrina* (see question 4 of the *prima pars*). Thus from a point near the end of the *Summa Theologiae*, one returns—as one must—to its beginning.

Chapter 4

The Whole Mystery of Our Salvation: Saint Thomas Aquinas on the Eucharist as Sacrifice

Bruce D. Marshall

PART I

"In this sacrament," says Saint Thomas of the Eucharist, "is included the whole mystery of our salvation."[1] This observation comes at the outset of a detailed commentary on the Mass, a "mystagogical" analysis of the Eucharistic rite which concludes the *Summa Theologiae*'s questions on the sacrament of the altar (III, q. 83, aa. 4–6).[2] Thomas's analysis of "the things which are said" and "the things which are done in the celebration of this mystery" (III, q. 83, pro.) reinforces a point he has already made: the Eucharist is at once a sacrament and a sacrifice. If we are to understand the way in which the whole mystery of our salvation is included in the Eucharist, we need to grasp

---

1. *Summa Theologiae*, III, q. 83, a. 4, c.: "in hoc sacramento totum mysterium nostrae salutis comprehenditur" (reading "totum" [Leonine] for "tantum" in the Blackfriars edition). For just this reason, Saint Thomas immediately goes on to observe, "prae caeteris sacramentis cum maiori solemnitate agitur." On this see the study by Sister Thomas Augustine Becker, OP, in this volume.

All translations are my own; unless otherwise noted those from the *Summa Theologiae* follow the Latin text in the Blackfriars edition.

2. For the use of the term *mystagogy* here, together with a close reading of these texts, see Franck Quoëx, "Thomas d'Aquin, mystagogue: L'*expositio missae* de la *Somme de théologie* (III, q. 83, aa. 4–5)," *Revue thomiste* 105 (2005): 179–224, 435–472. See also David Berger, *Thomas Aquinas and the Liturgy*, trans. Christopher Grosz (Naples, FL: Sapientia Press, 2005), 27–41.

both the sense in which the Eucharist is a sacrament and the sense in which it is a sacrifice, and we need also to see how the two are inseparably connected.

That is a far taller order than I can fill here. I will simply try to sort out what Saint Thomas means when he says that the Eucharist is a sacrifice, and address a few questions that come up along the way. There are questions aplenty, stemming from the fact that the Eucharist, uniquely among the seven sacraments, is also a sacrifice.[3]

However closely sacrament and sacrifice are connected in the mystery of the Eucharist, Saint Thomas nonetheless sees them as irreducibly distinct from one another. This is evident not only from the fact that he often makes a verbal distinction between them, but from the fact that he sees these two aspects of the Eucharist as having different *rationes* or concepts, tied to different effects. The Eucharist satisfies the concept of a sacrament, Thomas observes, insofar as it is received or consumed, while it satisfies the concept of a sacrifice insofar as it is offered (cf. III, q. 79, a. 5, c). Its sacramental effects are therefore limited to those who are actually present to taste it, while its sacrificial effects may extend to those for whom it is offered, even if they are not present to receive it, or, indeed, no longer present in this world at all (cf. III, q. 79, a. 7). So while the Eucharist is at once (*simul*: III, q. 79, a. 5, c) sacrament and sacrifice, the concepts of "sacrament" and "sacrifice" each do their own work in our understanding of it. Neither can be eliminated in favor of the other.

Many commentators have observed that Thomas's treatment of the Eucharist as sacrifice is remarkably modest when compared to his discussion of the Eucharist as sacrament. Aquinas gives a massive account, theologically, semantically, and metaphysically rich, of the Eucharist as a sacrament—as a sensible sign and instrumental cause of the grace of Christ in us, unique and supreme among the sacraments in fully containing the reality of which it is a sign; namely, the whole Christ himself (thus, e.g., III, q. 73, a. 1, ad 3; q. 75, a. 1; q. 76, a. 1). By contrast there is only one article in the entire Thomasian corpus devoted directly to Eucharistic sacrifice: *Summa Theologiae*, III, q. 83, a. 1, on "whether Christ is immolated in the celebration of

---

3. Thus, III, q. 79, a. 7, ad 1: "hoc sacramentum prae aliis habet quod est sacrificum."

this mystery" (following the title in III, q. 83, pro.). We naturally wonder about the reasons for this apparent imbalance.

Peter Lombard takes up Eucharistic sacrifice in Book IV, distinction 12, of the *Sentences*. He there succinctly gathers much of the matter, lexical and textual, basic to later scholastic reflection on the Eucharist, prompted by the question of "whether what the priest does is properly called a sacrifice or immolation, and whether Christ is immolated daily, or was only immolated once."[4] To this question he answers, after introducing several patristic texts, that "what is done on the altar is, and is called, a sacrifice. Christ both was offered once, and is offered daily, but in one way then, and in another way now."[5] The *unity* of that sacrifice in which the mystery of our salvation consists evidently worries the Lombard, as it would many after him. How is it that the sacrifice Christ offers once for all on Calvary, and the sacrifice the Church offers daily in the celebration of the Eucharist, are finally not two different offerings, but one and the same sacrifice? Peter Lombard suggests some limits to be observed in reflection on this mat-ter, some rules to follow. Christ's saving sacrifice on Calvary is a "once for all" (*semel*) action, unique and unrepeatable; the Church's daily Eucharistic action is a genuine sacrifice, in which Christ is truly offered; the offering of Christ takes place in one way on Calvary, and in another way on the altar (*aliter tunc, aliter nunc*). Lombard goes no further: we must observe these limits, but how we can do so he does not say.

This question may seem quite basic to us, and we might expect Aquinas to tackle it head on. Yet when Thomas gets to Book IV, distinction 12, in his own *Scriptum* on the *Sentences*, he offers no article, not even a passing *quaestiuncula*, on sacrifice, though the *expositio textus* of this distinction does take up the issue briefly in a treatment of the Eucharistic rite, and it sometimes crops up elsewhere (in connection, for example, with the question on why there are two distinct Eucharistic elements).[6] In his lack of concern about the

---

4. *Magistri Petri Lombardi Sententiae in IV Libris Distinctae*, IV, 12, 5 (3rd ed. [Grottaferrata: Editiones Collegii S. Bonaventurae Ad Claras Aquas, 1981], vol. 2, pp. 308–9; the quoted passage is p. 308.14–15).

5. "Ex his colligitur sacrificium esse et dici, quod agitur in altari; et Christum semel oblatum, et quotidie offerri; sed aliter tunc, aliter nunc" (*Sententiae* IV, 12, 5 [4], p. 309.22–4).

6. *In* IV *Sent.* 12, §§ 267–276 (=*Scriptum super libros Sententiarum*, vol. 4, ed. M. F. Moos [Paris: Lethielleux, 1947], pp. 539–41). Saint Thomas's discussion here focuses mainly on the

theology of Eucharistic sacrifice, however, Aquinas is not original. Saint Bonaventure, whose commentary on the *Sentences* Saint Thomas evidently had before him in the composition of his own, devotes even less explicit attention to sacrifice than Thomas does, at precisely the textual point in Lombard where we would expect an interest in the sacrificial aspect of the Eucharist to emerge.[7] Thomas, it seems, does not so much deliberately ignore the sacrificial side of the Eucharist as follow an established pattern that does not see this as a problem needing special attention.

One obvious reason for this seeming disinterest in the theology of Eucharistic sacrifice—to what extent this suggestion is actually correct I will not try to decide here—is simply that the sacrificial character of the Eucharist had never been contested in the Western Church (or the Eastern, for that matter) at the time when Bonaventure and Aquinas wrote. By contrast the real presence, and the way in which the bread and wine on the altar are (or are not) transformed into Christ's true body and blood, had been a regular subject of theological dispute in the West for several hundred years, and two centuries after the fact scholastic theologians at the time of Aquinas remain quite conscious of the need not to go where Berengar had gone on this matter (see, e.g., III, 75, 1, c). Sacrifice, unaccompanied by a large existing body of disputed questions calling for an answer, can be taken up where it comes up, often in passing (for example, in discussions of the *ritus* appropriate to the Eucharist).

Of course the sacrificial character of the Eucharist did become contested later on. Even before the Reformation a lively debate arose, prompted by the great increase in Masses for the dead and the living ("private" Masses), over whether each Mass is, like the cross itself, of infinite sacrificial value, or whether it has only limited sacrificial

---

ways in which the gestures of the priest represent the Passion of Christ: "Sacerdos enim non solum verbis, sed etiam factis Christi passionem repraesentat" (§ 268 [p. 540]). On the duality of Eucharistic elements signifying Christ's Passion, cf. *In* IV *Sent.* 11, 2, 1, i, sol (§ 148 [p. 460]).

7. See Bonaventure, *In* IV *Sent.* 12, pt. II, dubia 1–3 (*S. Bonaventurae Opera Omnia* [Quaracchi: Ex Typographia Collegii S. Bonaventurae, 1882–1902] vol. 4, pp. 298–9). For more on Eucharist and sacrifice among immediate predecessors well known to Thomas (the *Summa Halesiana*, William of Auvergne, Bonaventure, and Albert the Great), see Marius Lepin, *L'Idée du sacrifice de la messe: d'après les théologiens depuis l'origine jusqu'a nos jours*, 3rd ed. (Paris: Beauchesne, 1926), 164–82. On Thomas's use of Bonaventure (and Albert) in the composition of the *Scriptum*, cf. Jean-Pierre Torrell, OP, *St. Thomas Aquinas*, vol. 1, *The Person and His Work*, 2nd ed. (Washington, DC: The Catholic University of America Press, 2005), 44–5.

weight.[8] The Reformation greatly extended and intensified these debates. Reaching back to the sixteenth century there is a huge controversial literature regarding the Eucharist as sacrifice, on the one hand (between Catholics and Protestants) about whether the Mass is a sacrifice at all, and if so, whether it is a sacrifice that actually takes away sins, and on the other hand (mainly among Catholic theologians themselves) about how to conceive the unity of the sacrifice of the Mass with the sacrifice on Calvary, and of both with Christ's offering in the upper room at the institution of the Eucharist.[9]

But Thomas's comparative brevity on this point should not, I think, lead us to suppose that he regards sacrifice as a secondary, let alone insignificant, feature of the Eucharist. Despite the disparity in his treatment of the two, Thomas seems to regard "sacrament" and

---

8. Thus Gabriel Biel, whose *Canonis Missae Expositio* of 1488 is the most extensive late medieval reflection on the Eucharist, picks up an established train of argument for the inherently finite merit or sacrificial value of each Mass; see, e.g., lectio XXVII, esp. K-L (*Gabrielis Biel Canonis Missae Expositio*, eds. Heiko A. Oberman and William J. Courtenay [Wiesbaden: Franz Steiner Verlag, 1963–7], vol. 1, 264–6). Cajetan argues from a Thomist perspective against Biel and others that each Mass is inherently or objectively of infinite worth, though its effects are limited by the intentions of the celebrant and the receptivity of those for whom it is intended. Thus both defend the multiplication of Mass intentions, but on the basis of sharply opposed understandings of Eucharistic sacrifice. For a translation of Cajetan's disputed question (1510) on "The Celebration of the Mass," see Heiko A. Oberman, ed., *Forerunners of the Reformation: The Shape of Late Medieval Thought*, trans. Paul J. Nyhus (New York: Holt, Rinehart, and Winston, 1966), 256–64; on the argument between Cajetan and Biel, cf. Oberman's introduction, pp. 243–55. The presenting question—whether a priest who celebrates a single Mass for more than one person fulfills his obligation to each of them—had already been identified by Scotus, and treated as the occasion for reflection (along the lines that Biel would later follow) on the sacrificial significance of the Mass. Cf. *Quaestiones Quodlibetales*, 20, in English as John Duns Scotus, *God and Creatures: The Quodlibetal Questions*, eds. and trans. Felix Alluntis, OFM, and Allan B. Wolter, OFM, 2nd ed. (Washington, DC: The Catholic University of America Press, n.d.), 443–68.

9. On the complex history of these debates, see (from various dogmatic and theological points of view) Darwell Stone, *A History of the Doctrine of the Holy Eucharist*, vol. 2 (London: Longmans, Green, 1909); Lepin, *L'Idée du sacrifice de la messe*; "Messe: III. Le sacrifice de la Messe dans l'Église latine du IVe siècle jusqu'à la veille de la Réforme (A. Gaudel), IV. La Messe durant la période de la Réforme et du concile de Trente (J. Rivière), V. La Messe chez les théologiens postérieurs au concile de Trente (A. Michel)," *Dictionnaire de théologie catholique* 10/1 (1928), 964–1316; Burkhard Neunheuser, *Eucharistie in Mittelalter und Neuzeit* (Freiburg: Herder, 1963); Kenneth W. Stevenson, *Eucharist and Offering* (New York: Pueblo, 1986); James T. O'Connor, *The Hidden Manna: A Theology of the Eucharist*, 2nd ed. (San Francisco: Ignatius Press, 2005). For ecumenically attentive approaches to the same history, see Paul C. Empie and T. Austin Murphy, eds., *The Eucharist as Sacrifice*, in idem, *Lutherans and Roman Catholics in Dialogue I-III* (Minneapolis: Augsburg, 1974); Karl Lehmann and Edmund Schlink, eds., *Das Opfer Jesu Christi und seine Gegenwart in der Kirche: Klarungen zum Opfercharakter des Herrenmahles* (Freiburg: Herder & Göttingen: Vandenhoeck & Ruprecht, 1983).

"sacrifice" as equally basic to our understanding of the Eucharist. He clearly distinguishes the two concepts, and then pairs them in his account of the Eucharist, and in particular of its effects and its celebration. That he says less about sacrifice than about the real presence means not that he thinks it is less important, but only that to him and his time it seems less problem-laden.

How, then, does Saint Thomas understand the Eucharist to be a sacrifice, and in what way is "the whole mystery of our salvation" included in this sacrifice?

Part II

Reflection on the perfect sacrifice of Jesus Christ provides Saint Thomas with an opportunity to clarify the nature of sacrifice in general. "In the most basic sense, a 'sacrifice' is that which is done in order to please God, by giving God the honor owed uniquely to him" (III, q. 48, a. 3, c.).[10] *What* Christ offers for the honor of God is his own human flesh, "which is the most perfect sacrifice."[11] Christ's flesh is supremely fit to be offered as a sacrifice pleasing to the Father, because it is the human flesh of God the Son himself, and as such, invested with an infinite worth.[12] The offering of this flesh is specifically a sacrifice, as opposed to other kinds of offering, because it is

---

10. "Sacrificium proprie dicitur aliquid factum in honorem proprie Deo debitum, ad eum placandum." *Ad eum placandum*: "in order to please," but also "in order to placate" (cf. III, q. 49, a. 4, c.: by Christ's sacrifice, "Deus placatus est super omni offensa generis humani."). At the most elemental level sacrifice not only honors God, but acknowledges the sacrificing creature's subjection to him; it is offered "in signum debitae subiectionis et honoris (II-II, q. 85, a. 1, c.). So also Christ's saving sacrifice, like all his human acts (viz., all the acts he undertakes *secundum quod homo*) expresses his genuine subjection to the Father, a subjection the eternal Son himself accepts when he takes on our human flesh: "etiam Filius Dei, Philipp. [2:7], dicitur formam servi accipiens" (III, q. 20, a. 1, c.). This is a subjection of the very person or hypostasis of the Son, on account of his human (but not his divine) nature. "[P]roprie dici quod aliqua hypostasis vel persona sit domina vel serva secundum hanc vel illam naturam. Et secundum hoc, nihil prohibet Christum dicere Patri subjectum, vel servum, secundum humanam naturam" (ad 2).

11. III, q. 48, a. 3, ad 1: "carnem Christi, quae est perfectissimum sacrificium." A passage where Augustine reflects on the perfection of Christ's sacrifice (*De Trinitate* IV.xiv.19; *CCSL* 50, pp. 186.15–17) regularly furnished medieval theologians with a list of four elements essential to any sacrificial act: to whom it is offered, by whom it is offered, what is offered, and for whom it is offered. Cf. III, q. 22, a. 3, ad 1.

12. The value of Christ's flesh is to be reckoned "inquantum . . . erat caro Dei, ex quo habebat dignitatem infinitam" (III, q. 48, a. 2, ad 3). Here the idea of sacrifice overlaps with the closely connected notion of satisfaction; cf., regarding the Eucharist, III, q. 79, a. 5, c.: "Inquantum vero est sacrificium, habet vim satisfactivam."

immolated, that is, devoted to destruction.[13] The sacrificial offering of Christ's flesh thus takes place precisely in his Passion, which makes of the Passion itself "the sacrifice most pleasing to God" (*sacrificium Deo acceptissimum*; III, q. 49, a. 4, c.). Here the supreme sacrifice exhibits in its own way a characteristic of sacrifice in general: human acts "are properly called 'sacrifices' when something is done to that which is offered to God, for example that animals were killed, or that bread is broken and eaten and blessed" (II-II, q. 85, a. 3, ad 3).[14]

Jesus' Passion is a sacrifice, however, not only on account of what is offered and what happens to the offering, but on account of the interior disposition with which he offers it. In his suffering and death, Aquinas often observes, Jesus offers his own flesh to the Father freely, and out of the greatest possible love for the Father and for us (*ex caritate maxima*). For just this reason, he offers that sacrifice which is supremely pleasing to God (*Deo maxime acceptum*).[15]

Here, too, that which is highest in the genus of sacrifice displays a necessary feature of all sacrifice. The purpose of sacrifice is that human beings honor God and willingly subject themselves to him. This honor and subjection are first of all an inward act and disposition; they constitute "that interior spiritual sacrifice, by which the soul offers itself to God" (II-II, q. 85, a. 2, c.).[16] Jesus makes this interior offering in his perfect love for God, which is, as such, the heart of his sacrifice. But since we are fleshly beings, our interior acts are always tied to the material world, which touches us by our senses. Our interior sacrifice must be embodied, therefore, by the offering of a suitable material reality, to which "something is done." The very possibility of interior union with God depends for us on this bond of our inward honor and subjection with an exterior offering, which serves as its appropriate sign. "In order to be joined to God, the human mind needs the guidance of sensible things, . . . as the apostle

---

13. Cf. III, q. 48, a. 3, ad 1: "quia . . . erat [caro] passibilis et mortalis, apta erat immolationi."

14. In contrast to sacrifice, other kinds of oblation leave what is offered to God whole and unchanged: "[S]i aliquid exhibeatur in cultum divinum quasi in aliquod sacrum quod inde fieri debeat consumendum, et oblatio est et sacrificium. . . . Si vero sic exhibeatur ut integrum maneat . . . erit oblatio et non sacrificium" (II-II, q. 86, a. 1, c.).

15. "[H]oc ipsum quod [Christus] voluntarie passionem sustinuit, Deo maxime acceptum fuit, utpote ex caritate maxima proveniens" (III, q. 48, a. 3, c.; cf. ad 1; and q. 49, a. 4, c.).

16. Cf. II-II, q. 81, a. 7, c.: "per hoc quod Deum reveremur et honoramus, mens nostra ei subiicitur, et in hoc eius perfectio consistit."

says in Romans [1:20]."[17] Thus the infinite value of the exterior offering Jesus Christ makes (his flesh), perfectly matches the love he has in making it. For this reason his Passion is the "true sacrifice" (III, q. 48, a. 3, c.), of which any other sacrifice can at best be a shadow or figure, a representation or remembrance.

PART III

That the Eucharist, too, is a sacrifice, Saint Thomas, like the long tradition before him, regards as obvious. It is not simply an offering, as money or bread devoted to God on the altar can be an offering (cf. II-II, q. 85, a. 3, ad 3), but a genuine sacrifice, in which an immolation takes place each time the Eucharist is celebrated. Thomas sums up the matter by quoting a standard text, which the Lombard and Gratian attribute to Augustine: "Christ was sacrificed [*immolatus*] once for all in himself, and yet he is sacrificed [*immolatur*] each day in the sacrament" (III, q. 83, a. 1, s.c.).[18]

As this medieval commonplace suggests, a theological account of the Eucharist as sacrifice will have at least two basic rules to follow, or boundaries within which it must work. Peter Lombard had already sensed both, and Aquinas takes them for granted. On the one hand, the Eucharist itself is a sacrifice, which is offered "each day," that is, as often as the Mass is celebrated. "As often as we celebrate the memory of this victim," Thomas can say (citing a silent prayer of the celebrant for the ninth Sunday of Pentecost), "the work of our redemption is carried out."[19] As a result, "with several Masses

---

17. II-II, q. 81, a. 7, c.: "Mens autem humana indiget ad hoc quod coniungatur Deo, sensibilium manuductione: quia 'invisibilia per ea quae facta sunt, intellecta, conspiciuntur,' ut Apostolus dicit, ad Rom. Et ideo in divino cultu necesse est aliquibus corporalibus uti, ut eis, quasi signis quibusdam, mens hominis excitetur ad spirituales actus, quibus Deo coniungitur"; cf. II-II, q. 85, a. 1, c.; q. 84, a. 2, c.

18. The passage is actually paraphrased from Augustine's *Ep.* 98, and was introduced into the medieval discussion by Berengar. Cf. Lombard, *Sententiae* IV, 12, 5 (2) (p. 309.5–6, and note 1).

19. III, q. 83, a. 1, c.: "[I]n quadam dominicali oratione secreta dicitur: 'Quoties huius hostiae commemoratio celebratur, opus nostrae redemptionis exercetur.'" Just because each Mass enacts the work of our redemption, in the Eucharist "participes efficimur fructus dominicae passionis" (ibid.). On this text and its implications, see Benoît-Dominique de La Soujeole, op, "La présence dans les saints mystères: reflections à propos du *présent* christologique de l'eucharistie," *Revue thomiste* 104 (2004): 395–419, especially 397–8. On the "Roman-Franciscan" liturgy which serves as the basis for Thomas's commentary on the Mass in III, q. 83, see Quoëx, "Thomas d'Aquin, mystagogue," 206–210.

the offering of the sacrifice is multiplied, and therefore the effects of the sacrament and the sacrifice are also multiplied" (III, q. 79, a. 7, ad 3). On the other hand, the sacrifice offered in the Eucharist is Christ's own sacrifice, which he made only once, on Calvary, for the salvation of the world. The Eucharistic sacrifice is not, therefore, a second (or third, or fourth . . .) offering to be numbered alongside the once-for-all sacrifice which is Christ's Passion, but is the same as—one with—that unique saving oblation. "The sacrifice which is offered each day in the Church is not a different sacrifice from the one which Christ himself offered."[20]

In theological reflection on the mysteries of the faith, the rules are often easier to state than to follow. So it is here. How can one and the same sacrifice be multiplied? How can an unrepeatable sacrifice, a saving event that takes place once and for all, be offered or enacted daily in the Church? Aquinas, it has to be said, does not seem especially troubled by this classic conundrum, upon which Eucharistic theology since the sixteenth century has expended so much energy, and about which medieval theology before him had already begun to worry. He evidently thinks the conceptual joint between the sacrifice Christ offers once "in himself" and daily "in the sacrament" is not difficult to locate.

As Saint Thomas sees it, the concept of "representation" readily links the sacrifice of the Mass to the sacrifice of the cross. "This sacrament is called a 'sacrifice' insofar as it represents [*repraesentat*] the very passion of Christ" (III, q. 73, a. 4, ad 3; cf., e.g., q. 79, a. 1, c.; q. 79, a. 7, c.). This, too, is a medieval commonplace, traceable to Augustine.[21] The language of "representation" remains central to

---

Recent Magisterial teaching has underlined this insistence that the Mass itself "carries out" the one work of redemption. Thus Vatican Council II, *Lumen Gentium*, 3: "As often as the sacrifice of the cross by which 'Christ our Pasch is sacrificed' (1 Corinthians 5:7) is celebrated on the altar, the work of our redemption is carried out (*exercetur*)." Cf. John Paul II, *Ecclesia de Eucharistia*, 11: "When the Church celebrates the Eucharist, the memorial of her Lord's death and resurrection, this central event of salvation becomes really present and 'the work of our redemption is carried out.'"

20. "Sacrificum autem, quod quotidie in Ecclesia offertur, non est aliud a sacrificio quod ipse Christus obtulit" (III, q. 22, a. 3, ad 2)—to which Thomas adds, "sed eius commemoratio" (on which more momentarily).

21. Thus the Lombard: "[I]llud quod offertur et consecratur a sacerdote vocari sacrificium et oblationem, quia memoria est et repraesentatio sacrificii veri et sanctae immolationis factae in ara crucis." *Sententiae* IV, 12, 5 (1) (p. 308.15–18). He then cites Augustine on Ps. 20 (21; cf. *CCL*

later medieval discussions of Eucharistic sacrifice, and acquires dogmatic force at the Council of Trent.[22] The problem is to figure out what it means.

In Thomas, as in the broader medieval discussion of Eucharistic sacrifice, *repraesentatio* has a number of cognates which help to fill out its sense: the Eucharist is a *commemoratio* of Christ's once-for-all sacrifice (III, q. 22, a. 3, ad 2; q. 73, a. 4, c.; q. 83, a. 1, c.), a "recollection" (*recordatio*) of the Lord's death (III, q. 83, a. 1, c., citing Chrysostom as Ambrose), a *memoriale* of the Lord's Passion (III, q. 73, a. 5, ad 3; q. 79, a. 7, ad 2), a "sign" (*quoddam signum*) of it (III, q. 79, a. 6, c.), and an *exemplum* (III, q. 83, a. 1, ad 1; a. 2, c.) or "image" (*imago quaedam*) of the Passion (III, q. 83, a. 1, c.).[23] As Thomas's reliance on notions pertaining to memory suggests (following the language of the institution narratives and the Mass), the Eucharist "represents" the sacrifice of Christ by signifying or referring to a past event; namely, his Passion.[24] And the Eucharist is itself a sacrifice just by being the representation or image of this past event. "The celebration of this sacrament is a kind of image representing the passion of Christ [*imago quaedam . . . representativa*], which is his

---

38, 121): the remembrance (*recordatio*) of Christ's Passion "repraesentat quod olim factum est" (309.3–4).

22. See, e.g., Biel, *Canonis Missae Expositio*, lectio XXVII, K (Oberman and Courtenay, vol. 1, p. 265), and lectio LIII, U (vol. 2, p. 332); and the discussions in Gaudel, "Le sacrifice de la Messe dans l'Église latine," 1073–4; and Heiko A. Oberman, *The Harvest of Medieval Theology*, 3rd ed. (Durham, NC: Labyrinth Press, 1983), 271–80. According to Trent's *doctrina* on the sacrifice of the Mass (session XXII), Christ left to his Church at the Last Supper a "visibile (sicut hominum natura exigit) . . . sacrificium, quo cruentum illud semel in cruce peragendum repraesentaretur" (ch. 1; DH §1740).

23. Aquinas follows Lombard in attributing to Ambrose an important and frequently cited text on the Eucharist as a *recordatio* of Christ's death (cf. *Sententiae* IV, 12, 5 [3], p. 309), it stems, in fact, from Chrysostom's sermons on Hebrews 10. Cf. below, p. 56.

24. "[H]oc sacramentum habet triplicem significationem. Unam quidem respectu praeteriti: inquantum scilicet est commemorativum Dominicae passionis, quae fuit verum sacrificium. . . . Et secundum hoc nominatur 'sacrificium'" (III, q. 73, a. 4, c.).

On Aquinas's use of "representation" and associated concepts to understand the Eucharist as sacrifice, see Thierry-Dominique Humbrecht, OP, "L'eucharistie, «représentatio» du sacrifice du Christ, selon saint Thomas," *Revue thomiste* 98 (1998): 355–86, though I handle the question here somewhat differently from the way he does. Humbrecht depends in part on the discussion of the Eucharist as representation in Dom Anscar Vonier, *A Key to the Doctrine of the Eucharist* (1925; Bethesda, MD: Zaccheus Press, 2004).

true immolation. And for this reason the celebration of the sacrament is said to be the immolation of Christ" (III, q. 83, a. 1, c.; cf. ad 2).[25]

There is nothing *inherently* sacrificial, Aquinas here seems to say, about the words and deeds of the Church's Eucharist. The Eucharist is a sacrifice, to be sure, but it is so wholly in virtue of its reference to the once-for-all sacrifice of Calvary, a reference Aquinas sums up in the concept of "representation." The Eucharist is a true immolation, and thus a sacrifice, at all (it satisfies the *ratio* of an acceptable sacrifice) not in its own right, but only because of this reference. What makes the Eucharist acceptable to God, Thomas suggests, is that Christ himself is ultimately both its priest and victim, the one who offers and what is offered. For just this reason, but not otherwise, the Eucharist is nothing less than "the immolation of Christ," Christ's own sacrifice.

Saint Thomas is quite explicit about ways in which the celebration of the Eucharist "represents" the Passion of Christ. This only stands to reason, if the sacrificial character of the Eucharist depends on its being an "unbloody" representation of the "bloody sacrifice" of Christ, once offered (to recall the language of Trent and the modern literature on the subject).[26] Above all, the Eucharistic rite represents or commemorates the Passion of Christ by the double consecration, that is, by the transformation of the contents of the chalice into Christ's true blood, separate from the transformation of the bread into Christ's true body. "The blood consecrated separately explicitly [*expresse*] represents the passion of Christ," and for this reason, Aquinas goes on to observe, express mention of Christ's Passion and its saving fruits comes in the words for the consecration of the blood rather than those for the body (III, q. 78, a. 3, ad 2; cf. ad 1, ad 7).

Eucharistic concomitance, he takes care to note, is no obstacle to the representative significance of the double consecration. Though the whole Christ is present under each species, the double consecration is not a waste of time. On the contrary: the chalice is consecrated

---

25. Following the Leonine edition of the Tertia Pars, the Blackfriars text omits this last sentence ("And . . . Christ": *Et ideo celebratio huius sacramenti dicitur Christi immolatio*), but other editions retain it; I cite it here from the *Deutsche Thomas-Ausgabe*, vol. 30, *Das Geheimnis der Eucharistie* (III, qq. 73–83) (Salzburg & Leipzig: Verlag Anton Pustet, 1938), 324. In either case the sentence nicely summarizes the point of the argument that precedes it.

26. For Trent's use of these terms, cf. DH §1743.

separately "in order to represent the passion of Christ, in which his blood came to be separated from his body" (III, q. 76, a. 2, ad 1; cf. q. 74, a. 1, c.). This is the point, Aquinas again observes, of the sacrament's institution under this twofold form. "For this reason, the form for the consecration of the blood mentions its effusion" (q. 76, a. 2, ad 1). Christ is present in the Eucharist precisely as he is represented by it, as the one who offered once-for-all the sacrifice perfectly acceptable to God, precisely by the outpouring of his blood.[27]

Thomas adduces further ways in which the Eucharistic actions and their setting represent Christ's Passion, many of them long standard in the tradition. The mixing of water with wine before the consecration is a suitable way to represent the Passion of Christ, from whose wounded side flowed blood and water (III, q. 74, a. 6, c.). The fraction is likewise a "a sign [*sacramentum*] of the Lord's passion, which took place in Christ's true body" (III, q. 77, a. 7, c.; cf. q. 83, a. 5, ad 7). The small portion of consecrated host cast into the chalice signifies our participation in Christ's Passion, and in a different way his betrayal by Judas (III, q. 83, a. 5, ad 9). "The altar is a representation of his cross" (III, q. 83, a. 1, ad 2), the priest in a way represents Christ himself (ad 3), and the linen corporal on which the consecration of the bread takes place represents the linen shroud in which Christ's body was buried (III, q. 83, a. 3, ad 7). The *Scriptum*'s brief commentary on the Eucharistic rite notes many more such representations, some of which recur in the *Summa Theologiae*.[28] The priest makes the Sign of the Cross three times over the gifts "in order to signify the threefold handing over of Christ, by God, Judas, and the Jews" (cf. III, q. 83, a. 5, ad 3), in extending his arms right after the consecration the priest "represents an image [*effigiem*] of the cross" (cf. III, q. 83, a. 5, ad 5), and so forth. In general: "regarding this sacrament, the Church decides on [*statuit*] that which more expressly represents the passion of Christ" (III, q. 83, a. 3, ad 7).

---

27. I owe the felicitous phrase "present as he is represented" to Paul Gondreau, who attributes it to Father Gilles Emery, OP.

28. See *In IV Sent.* 12, *exposito textus*, §§268–9 (ed. Moos, p. 540), from which the following two quotations are taken.

PART IV

It has often been noted that "representation" and the concepts that circle around it seem at best a weak way of upholding the conviction that the Eucharist itself is a sacrifice, indeed the very sacrifice of Christ. The example Thomas uses to explain how the Eucharist represents Christ's sacrifice brings out the problem. Drawing on a text of Augustine, he observes that we often call the images of people or objects by the names of what they represent. "Thus, when we see a tablet or a wall with a picture on it, we say, 'That is Cicero,' or 'That is Sallust' " (III, q. 83, a. 1, c.). So also, as Thomas goes on to say, the celebration of the Eucharist "is a kind of image representing the passion of Christ" (ibid.). But just as a wall with Cicero's picture on it is not really Cicero, so, it would seem, the Eucharistic representation of Christ's Passion is not really Christ's sacrifice itself. If this example explains what it means to say that the Eucharist "represents" the sacrifice of Christ, then apparently the Eucharist "is called the immolation of Christ" (ibid.) only by an obvious equivocation. It is not really the same as the sacrifice Christ made once on Calvary, any more than a picture of Cicero is the same as the Roman orator who wrote *De natura deorum*. This upholds the unity of Christ's saving sacrifice, of course, but only at the cost of violating another basic rule; the Eucharist is no longer Christ's own sacrifice.

Comparing the Eucharist with the Old Testament sacrifices, as Saint Thomas often does, further sharpens the problem. Thomas has a high view of the cultic practices of the "Old Law," which united faithful Israelites to the Passion of Christ yet to come, and in this way effected their justification and salvation.[29] They did this precisely by being representations, images, or likenesses—"figures" (*figurae*) is Thomas's usual term in this context—of Christ's future Passion. The ceremonies of the Old Law were evidently related to Christ's Passion before the fact in much the same way as the Eucharist is related after it. Since there can be no salvation without faith in the Passion of Christ, Aquinas argues,

---

29. "Poterat autem mens fidelium, tempore legis, per fidem coniungi Christo incarnato et passo: et ita ex fide Christi iustificabantur. Cuius fidei quaedam protestatio erat huiusmodi caeremoniarum observatio, inquantum erant figura Christi" (I-II, q. 103, a. 2, c.).

it was necessary that in every time there be some representation of the Lord's Passion [*aliquod repraesentativum Dominicae passionis*]. In the Old Testament the chief sacrament of the Passion was the paschal lamb. . . . In the New Testament this has been succeeded by the sacrament of the Eucharist, which is a remembrance of the Passion as a past event [*rememo- rativum praeteritae passionis*], just as the paschal lamb was a prefiguration of his Passion still to come [*praefigurativum futurae*].[30]

A number of the Old Testament ceremonies, including the Paschal lamb, were genuine sacrifices.[31] As divinely sanctioned immolations offered to the one true God in order to be united with him in a holy society, they fully satisfied the *ratio* of a sacrifice. As such they were inherently linked, by anticipation, to the Passion of Christ, which they represent. But for just this reason they are not the sacrifice of Christ. Because they are right sacrifices that represent or "figure" Christ's one saving sacrifice still to come, they must come to a halt once Christ has made his own perfect offering. The cultic practices of the Old Testament "represent" the sacrifice of Christ, in other words, precisely by being really (that is, numeri- cally) distinct from Christ's own sacrifice. Unlike the daily offering of the Eucharist—so, at least, Thomas says—the offering of the Paschal lamb is not the sacrifice of Christ itself. Rather, like the rest of the Old Testament cult, it is a shadow of the truth (following Colossians 2:17 and Hebrews 10:1). And when the truth comes, shadows and figures must give way. They must, in fact, cease altogether.[32]

---

30. III, q. 73, a. 5, c.; cf. q. 73, a. 6, on the Paschal lamb as the chief figure of the Eucharist itself.

31. On Thomas's classification of the ceremonial law into "sacrifices, sacred things, sacraments, and observances" (which is not original with him), see I-II, q. 101, a. 4.

32. Christ "came to take away the figures which he fulfilled, since he is the truth" (III, q. 66, a. 2, ad 2: "venerat sua veritate figuras impletas auferre"). Cf. I-II, q. 104, a. 6, ad 2: "lex vetus fuit figura novi testamenti, et ideo debuit cessare, veritate veniente," and, similarly, *In* IV *Sent.* 1, q. 2, a. 5, qla. 2, s.c. 1: "[D]icitur Heb. 10:1: umbram habet lex futurorum bonorum. Sed veniente veritate cessat figura. Ergo veniente Christo legalia cessare debuerunt" (ed. Moos, p. 62, § 293); cf. idem, sol. (Moos, p. 65, § 307).

The legitimacy of the ancient sacrifices is just what makes it impossible to continue them once the figured reality has come. As sacrifices instituted for a saving purpose, yet irreducibly distinct from Christ's own, they would now be offered in competition with Christ's one saving oblation. Thus Aquinas insists that the practice of the Mosaic ceremonies turns deadly (*mortifera*) after the coming of Christ; save in its moral dimension, the "Old Law" can no longer be observed without mortal sin (cf. I-II, q. 103, a. 4, c.). This, to be sure, raises important questions about the election of Israel and the sacramental economy of the Old and New Testaments, which I hope to explore in a forthcoming monograph on Christ and Israel in the theology of Aquinas.

Seen in this light, it becomes striking to recall that Aquinas explains how the Eucharist itself serves as a representation or commemoration by contrasting it with Christ's Passion, which is "the true sacrifice" (*quae fuit verum sacrificium*, III, q. 73, a. 4, c.; cf. q. 83, a. 1, c.: "vera eius immolatio"). Still more startling is his explanation for why we do not celebrate the Eucharist on Good Friday. The Eucharist, he says, is not only an image or representation, but "in a certain way, a figure [*figura quaedam*]" of Christ's Passion. As in other cases, "when the truth comes, the figure must cease." So on this day, when our recollection attends in a special way to the Lord's Passion "as it really happened," there is no consecration of the Eucharist; no figure present, only the reality recalled.[33]

Of course the practice of not celebrating the Eucharist on Good Friday was well established by the time of Saint Thomas. But in order to account for it, he invokes just the same principle that distinguishes Israel's sacrifices from Christ's Passion as shadow from reality, figure from truth: *veniente veritate, cessat figura*. In the context of Thomas's broader theology of sacrifice, the logic of "representation" and its cognates, far from tending to identify the Eucharist with Christ's own sacrifice, apparently drives a sharp wedge between the two.

At this point the temporal location of the Eucharist is decisive for its sacrificial character. Since they took place before the Passion of Christ, the sacrifices and other ceremonies of the Old Law "conferred" the grace they signify, but did not "contain" it. The sacraments of the New Law, because they take place in the temporal wake of Christ's Passion, actually contain the grace they signify. Aquinas spells out this difference in terms of the causal power of the rites. Israel's sacrifices were figures of Christ's future Passion, and as such they could act as final causes. By means of these rites, Christ acted in Israel as final cause, eliciting faith in his Passion yet to be, and so graciously

---

33. III, q. 83, a. 2, ad 2: "[V]eniente veritate, cessat figura. Hoc autem sacramentum est figura quaedam et exemplum dominicae passionis, sicut dictum est. Et ideo in die quo ipsa passio Domini recolitur, prout realiter gesta est, non celebratur consecratio huius sacramenti." Aquinas likewise contrasts the Eucharist and the Passion as "figure" and "truth" when he addresses, in *Quodlibet* V, 3, 2, c, the striking question whether the greater token of love on Christ's part is giving his body for us on the cross, or in the Eucharist. The Passion, he replies, is obviously the greater sign of love: "Vnde et hoc sacramentum est memoriale quoddam et figura passionis Christi; ueritas autem preminet figure et res memoriali" (Leonine ed., vol. 25/2, p. 371a, ll. 49-52).

joining Israel to himself in faith and love. The sacraments of the New Law, however, confer grace by an efficient causality which "flows into" them "from Christ incarnate and crucified," whose Passion must actually occur in order for the material signs to have this new potency.[34] A basic metaphysical principle comes into play here. Efficient causes, unlike final causes, cannot be later in time than what they move. As a result, Christ's Passion could not yet be operative in the ancient ceremonies as efficient cause, though it could as final cause. But once it has occurred, Christ's Passion can act as efficient cause, in virtue of which the Church's sacraments actually contain, as Christ's material instruments, the power to join us to him.[35]

The Eucharist, however, differs not only from the ceremonial law, but also from the rest of the Church's sacraments, on account of what it contains. While the other sacraments contain grace, that is, "an instrumental power communicated by Christ [*participata a Christo*]," the Eucharist contains "Christ himself, substantially" (III, q. 65, a. 3, c.; cf. q. 73, a. 1, ad 3: "*continet . . . ipsum Christum*"). More precisely, the Eucharist, as Thomas regularly says, contains *ipsum Christum passum*: the very Christ who suffered for us, Christ in his Passion. This makes it "the perfect sacrament of the Lord's passion," since it not only contains the saving causal efficacy which flows forth from his Passion, but the very flesh which was pierced by

---

34. "[Q]uia mysterium incarnationis et passionis Christi nondum erat realiter peractum, illae veteris legis caeremoniae non poterant in se continere realiter virtutem profluentem a Christo incarnato et passo, sicut continent sacramenta novae legis" (I-II, q. 103, a. 2, c.).

35. "Nihil autem prohibet id quod est posterius tempore, antequam sit, movere . . . sicut finis, qui est posterior tempore, movet agentem, secundum quod est apprehensus et desideratus ab ipso, sed illud quod nondum est in rerum natura, non movet secundum usum exteriorum rerum; unde causa efficiens non potest esse posterior in esse ordine durationis, sicut causa finalis. Sic ergo manifestum est quod a passione Christi, quae est causa humanae iustificationis, convenienter derivatur virtus iustificativa ad sacramenta novae legis, non autem ad sacramenta veteris legis" (III, q. 62, a. 6, c.). On the Passion of Christ as efficient cause of our salvation in the present, see also III, q. 48, a. 6, esp. ad 2: "per spiritualem contactum [passio Christi] efficaciam sortitur: scilicet per fidem et fidei sacramenta."

Thomas's idea that the Passion of Christ acts by way of the sacraments as an efficient cause in the present has puzzled many Thomists, since Christ's Passion is a completed event in the past and as such, so it would seem, cannot have causal efficacy once it is over—it is no longer actual, and so cannot act as an efficient cause. Suarez, for example, says of the passage just quoted, "Doctrina D. Thomae in hoc articulo difficilis plane est, nisi benigne explicetur" (cited in Charles Journet, *L'Église du Verbe incarné*, vol. 2, *Sa structure interne et son unite catholique*. Oeuvres completes de Charles Journet, vol. 2 [Éditions Saint-Augustin, 1999], p. 331 note 178; cf. p. 335 note 188, where Journet takes sharp issue with Suarez and others on the matter). To this we will return briefly at the end of this paper.

the nails and lance, not only the power to join us to Christ, but the Christ to whom we are joined.[36] As such, the Eucharist "could not be instituted before the incarnation"; indeed, doubly so. Not only would it lack the causal power to unite us to Christ, it would lack, even more, its own distinctive content—the very Christ who has borne his saving Passion.[37]

That the Eucharist contains *ipsum Christum passum* is pivotal, on Thomas's view, for understanding how it is a sacrifice. Here, too, he gains clarity by referring to the sacrifices of the Old Law, but now as a point of contrast. We can say that the sacrifices of the Old Law "contained" the one true sacrifice of Christ. They did so, however, only in the minimal sense that any figure can be said to contain another object or event; namely, by representing or referring to it, while the figured reality is not itself present in the figure. In keeping with the perfection of the new covenant, the "sacrifice of the new law instituted by Christ"—the Eucharist—must contain Christ's sacrifice in a more direct and intimate way. This it does precisely by containing Christ himself, "not only by way of signification or figure, but also in reality."[38] That it contains the very Christ who suffered as the true sacrifice for sin is just what distinguishes the Eucharist, as a sacrifice, from all the figural offerings of the Old Testament. Israel's sacrifices "contained" Christ's true immolation solely by figuring or representing

---

36. III, q. 73, a. 5, ad 2: "Eucharistia est sacramentum perfectum Dominicae passionis, tanquam continens ipsum Christum passum." The *Lectura* on John puts this same point the other way around. Since the Eucharist is the sacrament of the Lord's Passion, it must contain him in his suffering: "[C]um hoc sacramentum sit dominicae passionis, continent in se Christum passum" (*Super Ioannem* 6, 6 [§ 963]).

37. III, q. 73, a. 5, ad 2: because the Eucharist contains "ipsum Christum passum . . . ideo non potuit institui ante incarnationem: sed tunc habebant locum sacramenta quae erant tantum praefigurativa Dominicae passionis." Scotus later disagrees with this claim, and holds that the body of Christ, since it is by God's power equally capable of existing in its natural and its sacramental modes, could have been made present by God in the Eucharist before, and indeed without, Christ's Incarnation and Passion (though this is, of course, not the way God has actually ordered things). See Scotus, *Ordinatio* IV, d. 10, q. 4, especially §§ 4–6 (ed. Vivès, vol. 17, pp. 230b–232a.). An extensive debate over this question ensued between Scotists and Thomists; for a particularly caustic reply to Scotus, see Cajetan's commentary on *Summa Theologiae*, III, q. 76, a. 2 (ed. Leonine 12, pp. 181–2).

38. III, q. 75, a. 1, c.: "Sacrificia enim Veteris Legis illud verum sacrificium passionis Christi continebant solum in figura: secundum illud Heb. X, 'Umbram habens lex futurorum bonorum, non ipsam rerum imaginem.' Et ideo oportuit ut aliquid plus haberet sacrificium novae legis a Christo institutum; ut scilicet contineret ipsum passum, non solum in significatione vel figura, sed etiam in rei veritate."

a future Passion they could not contain in reality, while the Eucharist really contains it, by containing him.[39]

Similarly, the consecrated host can be called by that name (*hostia*—"victim") because it not only represents Christ's sacrifice, it contains the sacrificed Christ (cf. III, q. 73, a. 4, ad 3). As a result, "the true sacrifice of Christ"—nothing less—"is shared with the faithful under the species of bread and wine." Holy Communion therefore constitutes, as Augustine had already said, the Church's own "participation in the sacrifice of Christ."[40] By contrast, the Israelites in the desert "ate true spiritual food" (cf. 1 Corinthians 10:3–4): they fed on Christ spiritually—were united with him in faith and love—but not sacramentally, by tasting his true body (III, q. 80, a. 1, ad 3; cf. q. 83, a. 4, ad 8).

In the one article where Saint Thomas asks explicitly whether Christ is sacrificed in the Eucharist, the first objection, naturally enough, is that he cannot be, since scripture teaches (Hebrews 10:14) that he has made only one offering. The outcome of this oblation is eternal sanctification, and so it will never have to be repeated (cf. III, q. 83, a. 1, obj. 1). Thomas's reply to this objection is disconcertingly brief, and consists mostly of a quotation from Chrysostom, which Thomas attributes to Ambrose. But in light of Thomas's earlier argument that the Eucharist is itself a sacrifice because it contains *ipsum Christum passum*, the reply nonetheless suffices to make his point.

There is one victim, "that is, which Christ offered, and we offer," and not multiple victims. What Christ offered once in sacrifice was his own body, and this very same body the Eucharist now contains. When we now celebrate the Eucharist, therefore, we offer to the Father what Christ offered in his Passion: one and the same— numerically the same—body, the one body which is our eternal redemption. And so, Aquinas comments (using Chrysostom's words), our sacrifice is the same as his. "Just as there is one body which is offered everywhere, and not many bodies, so also there is one sacrifice,"

---

39. This I take to be the sense of Aquinas's remark, otherwise puzzling, that Christ "poterat dici . . . immolari etiam in figuris veteris Testamenti," and not only in the Eucharist (III, q. 83, a. 1, c.).

40. III, q. 22, a. 6, ad 2: The bread and wine of the Eucharist signify, "ut Augustinus dicit, 'ecclesiasticam unitatem, quam constituit participatio sacrificii Christi.' Unde etiam in nova lege verum Christi sacrificium communicatur fidelibus sub specie panis et vini." Cf. q. 48, a. 3 ad 1: Christ's human flesh "congrue pro hominibus offertur, et ab eis sumitur sub sacramento."

and not many sacrifices. In just this sense, "our sacrifice is an *exemplum*," or representation, "of his."[41] That is: much as we rightly say that a picture is Cicero, but do not count a picture of him as a second Cicero beside the one of flesh and blood, so also we say of the host that it is Christ's body given up (sacrificed) for us, and of the cup that it is Christ's blood poured out for us, without counting these as a second sacrifice beside that of Calvary. It is too easy simply to assume that "to represent" in Aquinas's Eucharistic theology means "to make [the same thing] present again," but that seems to be what it comes to in the end.

This gives us some initial purchase on the way in which the Eucharist, precisely as a sacrifice, includes "the whole mystery of our salvation." *What* we offer to God in the Eucharistic sacrifice is exactly the same as what Christ offered on Calvary for our salvation: his whole body and his outpoured blood. What he offered in his human nature is just what we now offer sacramentally, and in that sense, at least, our sacrifice is the same as his. Here Aquinas's theology of Eucharistic sacrifice depends closely on, without being reducible to, his theology of the Eucharist as sacrament, that is, as sign of the whole Christ whom it really contains.

PART V

To be sure, this is only half the story. A sacrifice includes not only something offered to God by way of immolation, but the act of offering it. Sacrifice always, and indeed for Aquinas primarily, has an interior as well as an exterior aspect. While the theology of the real presence gives us a way of saying that what we offer sacramentally is the same as what Christ offered on the cross, it still seems as though our *act* of offering must be distinct from his. The two take place, to note perhaps the most obvious distinctions, at different times and in different spaces. If our act of offering is finally distinct in number

---

41. III, q. 83, a. 1, ad 1: "[S]icut Ambrosius . . . dicit, 'una est hostia,' quam scilicet Christus obtulit, et nos offerimus, 'et non multae, quia *semel oblatus est Christus* [Heb 9:28], hoc autem sacrificum exemplum est illius. Sicut enim quod ubique offertur, unum est corpus, et non multa corpora, ita et unum sacrificum.'" Cf. *In Heb.* 10, 1, § 482: "[N]on offerimus aliam quam illam quam Christus obtulit pro nobis, scilicet sanguinem suum. Unde non est alia oblatio, sed est commemoratio illius hostiae quam Christus obtulit" (cited in Humbrecht, "Représentation," p. 370, note 32).

from Christ's own, then it means that our Eucharistic sacrifice is not
the same as Christ's one sacrifice after all, even though the two acts
have the same object or content.

How to think about the unity between Calvary and the
Eucharistic altar in the act of offering is, if anything, even more difficult than how to think about the unity in what is offered. Briefly,
though, Saint Thomas thinks of the Eucharist as Christ's own saving
act of sacrifice first of all by way of a theology of Christ's priesthood
and our participation in it.

The Church's Eucharistic act of sacrifice takes place when the
priest consecrates the bread and wine on the altar. "Sacrifice is offered
to God by the consecration of this sacrament."[42] This stands to reason,
since what the Eucharist offers to the Father—the body and blood
of Christ—comes to be present on the altar in virtue of the consecration. More precisely, the consecration completes or consummates
the Church's offering, while many words and deeds of the priest share,
as we have seen, in the act of representation which constitutes the
Eucharistic sacrifice.[43] The faithful, too, participate in the act of
offering in their own way. They do this chiefly by receiving, after the
priest, the offered body of Christ, but also by their joyous offering of
gifts for the altar, and their solemn assent to the act by which the
priest transforms their gifts into the perfect human sacrifice to God.[44]

---

42. III, q. 82, a. 10, c. Cf. q. 83, a. 4, c.: In the Canon of the Mass, the priest "consecrationem
peragit per verba Salvatoris," and then "petit hoc sacrificium peractum esse Deo acceptum." The
consecration of matter in the Eucharist thus differs from that in other sacraments, since in other
cases this act "non est sacrificium, sicut consecratio Eucharistiae" (q. 82, a. 4, ad 1).

43. In contrast to the other sacraments, as Aquinas often observes, the Eucharist is completed
(*perficitur*) not in the use the faithful make of the sacramental elements, but in their consecration
itself. The consecration suffices to bring it about that the Eucharistic elements fully contain the
holy reality they signify—Christ himself—whereas what the other sacraments signify (e.g., the
washing away of sin in Baptism) requires some use of a sacramental element by the faithful, or its
"application" to them (see, e.g., III, q. 73, a. 1, ad 3; q. 78, a. 1, c.). For this reason a priest can,
indeed should, celebrate the Eucharist even if he is not charged with the care of souls. "[A]lia
sacramenta perficiuntur in usu fidelium. . . . Sed hoc sacramentum perficitur in consecratione
Eucharistiae, in qua sacrificium Deo offertur, ad quod sacerdos obligatur Deo ex ordine iam
suscepto" (III, q. 82, a. 10, ad 1).

44. As the priest's participation in the act of sacrifice includes being the first to eat of the
sacrifice, so the faithful share in the sacrifice by eating the sacrificed body in their turn: the priest
"sacrificium populo dispensat," but "primo debet esse particeps. . . Per hoc autem fit particeps
quod de sacrificio sumit, secundum illud Apostoli I Cor. [10:18], 'Nonne qui edunt hostias,
participes sunt altaris?' " (III, q. 82, a. 4, c.). The offering of the Eucharistic sacrifice, and with
that the whole celebration of the Eucharistic mystery, begins with the sung praise of the people
in the Offertory, expressing the joy of those who make an offering (*laetitia offerentium*), followed

If the act (or acts) of priest and people in offering the Eucharistic sacrifice is not Christ's own act, then the Eucharist is not the same as the sacrifice of Christ. In that case the Eucharist would, despite Thomas's insistence, be another and different sacrifice, alongside the once-for-all offering made by Christ. Aquinas, however, does not think of the Church's act of sacrifice as discreet from Christ's own, but rather as included in Christ's saving act. As he often notes, the priest consecrates the Eucharist, and thereby offers the body and blood of Christ in sacrifice to the Father, not in his own person but in, or from (*ex*), the person of Christ. This does not simply mean that he is commissioned by Christ to carry out an act which he has no legal authority to undertake on his own, though that is right as far as it goes.[45] Even as commissioned for this sacramental act, the priest has no capacity of his own to carry it out. In order to be a genuinely sacramental act, one which confers the saving grace of Christ, the priest's act depends entirely on Christ's own agency (whether, of course, he thinks about this at the time or not).

This is true of all the sacraments, but is uniquely clear in the case of the Eucharist. In the other sacraments the words that make up the necessary "form" of the sacrament are uttered in the priest's own name, or in the first person, though their effectiveness depends on the action of Christ (in Baptism, for example, the priest says, "I baptize you . . ."). In the Eucharist, though, the words that form the sacrament "are uttered in the person of Christ himself as the speaker, by which we come to understand that in carrying out this sacrament, the minister does nothing, except utter the words of Christ."[46] The very form of the Eucharist makes it clear that the minister, considered as an individual human agent, does not consecrate the Eucharist. Christ

---

by the prayer of the priest that the people's offering might be acceptable to God (*ut oblatio populi sit Deo accepta*). The priest goes on to consecrate the *materia* the people have offered (all from III, q. 83, a. 4, c.), eliciting the "Amen" of the faithful to this sacrificial act undertaken for their good, which belongs to him alone (III, q. 83, a. 4, ad 6). On the role of the people in Thomas's understanding of the Eucharist, see Quoëx, "Thomas d'Aquin, mystagogue," 215–17, 444–7.

45. See, e.g., III, q. 82, a. 1, c.: "Quicumque autem aliquid agit in persona alterius, oportet hoc fieri per potestatem ab illo concessam."

46. III, q. 78, a. 1, c.: "Sed forma huius sacramenti profertur ex persona ipsius Christi loquentis: ut detur intelligi quod minister in perfectione huius sacramenti nihil agit nisi quod profert verba Christi."

does.[47] He is the one great high priest of every Eucharist, the living "source of all priesthood," whether that of the Levitical priest which anticipated him, or that of the priest who now acts, under the new covenant, in Christ's own person.[48] Jesus Christ, as Aquinas likes to say, is the primary agent (*agens principale*) of the Eucharist, as of all the sacraments. Both the priest himself and the words the priest utters are Christ's "instruments," dependent on him and his action for any sacramental effect they may have.[49] Indeed, the words of the Eucharist can have their effect, now as in the upper room, only as spoken by Christ himself. Christ is the source (*auctor*) of this sacrament, and the priest must use his very words to consecrate it, "since just as Christ gave his body up to death by his own will, so also he gives himself as food by his own power."[50] With consecration, as we have seen, goes sacrifice, so just as Christ is the *agens principale* of the priestly act of transubstantiation, so he is the *agens principale* of the Eucharistic sacrifice. The priest's sacrificial act is not a different act from Christ's own, but is the way Christ carries out his own sacrificial act here and now.

---

47. Cf. III, q. 75, a. 4, c.: the conversion of the substance of the bread into the body of Christ "non est similis conversionibus naturalibus, sed est omnino supernaturalis, sola Dei virtute effecta"; it lies beyond the capacity of any finite agent, but can take place "virtute agentis infiniti, quod habet actionem in totum ens" (ad 3). Just because what happens in this sacrament "a solo Deo perfici potest . . . minister in hoc sacramento perficiendo non habet alium actum nisi prolationem verborum" (q. 78, a. 1, c.).

48. "Christus autem est fons totius sacerdotii. Nam sacerdos legalis erat figura ipsius; sacerdos autem novae legis in persona ipsius operatur" (III, q. 22, a. 4, c.). Cf. *In Heb.* 7, 4 (§ 368): because his priesthood is eternal, "solus Christus est verus sacerdos, alii autem ministri eius."

49. On the priest and his words as instrumental causes in the Eucharist, with Christ as primary agent, see, e.g., III, q. 78, a. 4, ad 1–2; q. 82, a. 1, ad 1; *In Matt.* 26, 3 (§ 2181). Christ is, in general, "ipsa causa universalis omnium sacramentorum" (*Super Ioannem* 6, 6 [§ 964]), and his divinity and humanity found different kinds of primacy with respect to his sacramental causality (see III, q. 64, a. 3). Here some questions come into view regarding the notion of instrumental causality, especially when it comes to an "instrumentum animatum" (III, q. 64, a. 8, ad 1; cf. q. 62, a. 1, ad 2), in this case a priest: the instrument has a causality, and thus an act or movement, of its own, yet these are wholly dependent on the primary agent. But for present purposes we can leave these questions aside.

50. *Super Ioannem* 6, 6 (§ 961): "Auctor huius sacramenti Christus est: nam licet sacerdos consecret, tamen ipse Christus dat virtutem sacramento, quia etiam ipse sacerdos consecrat in persona Christi. Unde in aliis sacramentis utitur sacerdos verbis suis, seu Ecclesiae, sed in isto utitur verbis Christi: quia sicut Christus corpus suum propria voluntate dedit in mortem, ita sua virtute dat se in cibum." Similarly *In 1 Cor.* 11, 5 (§ 657): "sacerdos, dum consecrat, non profert ista verba quasi ex persona sua sed quasi ex persona Christi consecrantis"; see also III, q. 78, a. 1, ad 1.

Not only the priest, but all the faithful who celebrate the Eucharist, share in the priesthood of Christ, though in different ways. As Holy Orders give the priest the power (*potestas*) or capacity (*potentia*) to consecrate the Eucharist, so Baptism confers upon all the faithful the power or capacity to receive it.[51] Sacramental "character" is, in essence, the capacity to worship the one true God in Christ, to give or receive the divine goods imparted liturgically by the great high priest.[52] In fact, "the whole *ritus* of the Christian religion flows from the priesthood of Christ."[53] The Church's whole liturgy, embracing the particular powers and acts of both priest and people, is Christ's gift to us of a share in his own priesthood. Not only what we say, do, and offer in the Eucharist, but the very act of doing it, flows (or is "derived") from Christ himself, from his supreme priesthood. Thus the distinct sacramental characters conferred in Baptism and ordination "are in a special way the character of Christ, to whose priesthood the faithful are conformed by their sacramental characters, which are nothing other than ways of participating in the priesthood of Christ, which flow from Christ himself."[54]

Christ fully enacts his priesthood in his Passion (cf. III, q. 22, a. 5, obj. 2). This means not only that he offers himself on the cross "as a fragrant oblation and sacrifice to God" (Ephesians 5:2), but that by this offering he "inaugurates the worship which belongs to the Christian religion."[55] The Passion of Christ is not simply what Christian worship is *about*. Christ's Passion is *itself* the perfect Christian *ritus*, the perfect act of worship—of human offering to the Father. The Eucharistic actions for which Baptism and ordination

51. Thus III, q. 82, a. 1, c.: "Sicut autem baptizato conceditur a Christo potestas sumendi hoc sacramentum; ita sacerdoti cum ordinatur confertur potestas hoc sacramentum consecrandi in persona Christi."

52. "Divinus autem cultus consistit vel in recipiendo aliqua divina, vel in tradendo aliis." When it comes to the worship of God, therefore, "ad tradendum aliquid aliis requiritur quaedam potentia activa; ad accipiendum autem requiritur potentia passiva. Et ideo character importat quamdam potentiam spiritualem ordinatam ad ea quae sunt divini cultus" (III, q. 63, a. 2, c.).

53. "Totus autem ritus christiane religionis derivatur a sacerdotio Christi" (III, q. 63, a. 3, c.).

54. III, q. 63, a. 3, c.: "[C]haracter sacramentalis specialiter est character Christi, cuius sacerdotio configurantur fideles secundum sacramentales characteres, qui nihil aliud sunt quam quaedam participationes sacerdotii Christi ab ipso Christo derivatae." Cf. III, q. 22, a. 6, ad 2: the "excellence" of Christ's priesthood, in comparison with that of the Levitical cult, lies mainly in the depth to which the Church can participate in the sacrifice of this priest, and in its effect.

55. "[P]er suam passionem initiavit ritum christianae religionis, 'offerens seipsum oblationem et hostiam Deo,' ut dicitur Eph. 5." III, q. 62, a. 5, c.

equip Christ's people are a participation in his priesthood just because Christ grants us in the Eucharist a real share in his own priestly act, that is, in his Passion, which is the one perfect act of sacrifice to the Father.

PART VI

None of this yet answers the question of how our repeated Eucharistic sacrifice can be the same act as Christ's once-for-all sacrifice. But it helps to locate the real issue. The controversies of the Reformation era might prompt us to suppose that the main question is how to balance our action with Christ's, so that the Eucharist is not held to supplement or improve on Christ's own sacrifice. For Aquinas this question is already ill-formed, since he does not see our sacrifice and Christ's as two irreducibly discreet acts in the first place. Our act is not only causally dependent on, but (instrumentally) included in, Christ's own. Given this, we do not undertake in the Eucharist another act next to his, any more than we offer something besides what he offered (namely his body and blood).

The main difficulty, it seems, lies not in the relationship between Christ's act in the Eucharist and our own, but in the unity of Christ's sacrificial act itself. The hard problem, in other words, is not how Christ's priestly act in the Eucharist can be one with—the same as—our act, but how Christ's priestly act in the Eucharist can be one with—the same as—his own priestly act consummated on Calvary. After all "we know," as Saint Paul teaches, "that Christ being raised from the dead will never die again." His death took place in the past, "once for all," and now "he lives to God" in the full and eternal glory of the Father's only Son (Romans 6:9–10). That being the case, how can any act or event in the present, including an act of Christ himself, be the same as that effusion of his own blood unto death by which Christ once for all made the perfect sacrifice to the Father for us? The idea that Christ's sacrificial action in the Eucharist is the same as his sacrificial act on Calvary apparently attributes to him a property—the outpouring of his blood unto death—which he can no longer have; it seems inconsistent with basic Christian convictions about Jesus' present state, or, we could say, about his identity. The point can be put more broadly. It seems inconsistent to hold that one and the same act or event both has been completed in the past and takes place in the present.

Understandably puzzled at this point, Catholic theologians who have wanted a strong but consistent account of Eucharistic sacrifice have sometimes held that Christ's sacrificial act in the Eucharist cannot be the same as the sacrifice he completed once for all on the cross. What Christ's high-priestly act in the Eucharist makes present on the altar is not the whole of the sacrifice he completed on the cross for the life of the world, exactly, but some central part of it, which can plausibly be regarded as permanent. It is sometimes argued, for example, that Christ's sacrificial act as *agens principale* of the Eucharist consists chiefly in the outpouring of his charity, of that perfect love for the Father and for us which made the outpouring of his blood on Calvary the saving sacrifice. Since the Eucharist makes present Christ's own sacrificial love and invites us to share in it, we can rightly say that the Eucharist is a sacrifice. And since the charity Christ pours out in his present state of glory is presumably the same as the charity with which he underwent his Passion in the past, we can also rightly say that the Eucharist is, in a sense, Christ's one redemptive sacrifice.[56]

I will not here attempt to assess what merit this type of suggestion may have, still less to resolve the difficult problem of the unity of Christ's sacrifice on Calvary and on the altar. We may conclude, however, by observing that it will in any case be difficult to recruit Saint Thomas for a view of Eucharistic sacrifice on which anything less than the whole of Christ's once-for-all sacrifice on Calvary is present on the altar.

Commenting on John 6:51 (Vulg. 6:52: "the bread that I will give is my flesh for the life of the world"), Thomas pauses to consider the "usefulness" (*utilitas*) of the Eucharist. Just because the Eucharist contains Christ himself, in his Passion (*Christum passum*), we must recognize its singular usefulness for us: "For this sacrament is nothing other than the application of the Lord's passion to us." But the Lord's Passion only comes whole. The Eucharist does not apply to us simply the effects of the Lord's Passion, or one element of it rather than another. Rather, this sacrament applies to us—unites us in the present

---

56. Humbrecht, for example, seems to think about the matter along these lines. See "L'eucharistie, «représentatio» du sacrifice du Christ," 376–7.

to—the whole of the Lord's Passion. So much so, in fact, that "whatever is the effect of the Lord's passion, the whole of that is also the effect of this sacrament."[57] The Eucharistic sacrifice is evidently not a medium that imparts to us the saving effects of Christ's Passion (the destruction of death and the restoration of life, as Thomas here says), the way water, for example, can impart an electric shock. The Eucharist *has* the very same effects as the Passion itself. But the Eucharist can have these effects, can itself destroy death and impart life, only if it *is* the Passion, now applied to us. As Thomas insists, there are not two saving sacrifices, but only one. The sacrifice that was on Calvary then is on the altar now, though in a different mode; namely, as represented or commemorated by signs.[58] But the whole sacrifice of Christ, his act of offering as well as what he offers, is present now, and not only then.[59]

Thomas evidently means to be taken straight when he says that "the whole mystery of our salvation" is included in the Eucharist, as when he says—whether in the *Summa Theologiae* or at the altar—that "the work of our redemption," the very work accomplished once for all by Christ on Calvary, "is carried out as often as we celebrate" the Eucharist. How to understand this mysterious coincidence of past and present remains, to be sure, a difficult problem. But if we would be instructed by Saint Thomas on this matter, it is the right problem to have.

---

57. *Super Ioannem* 6, 6, (§ 963): "[C]um hoc sacramentum sit dominicae passionis, continet in se Christum passum: unde quidquid est effectus dominicae passionis, totum etiam est effectus huius sacramenti. Nihil enim aliud est hoc sacramentum quam applicatio dominicae passionis ad nos . . . Unde manifestum est quod destructio mortis, quam Christus moriendo destruxit, et reparatio vitae, quam resurgendo effecit, est effectus huius sacramenti." Cf. III, q. 79, a. 1, c.: Just because the Eucharist represents the Passion of Christ, "effectum, quem passio Christi fecit in mundo, hoc sacramentum facit in homine." Cf. also *Ecclesia de Eucharistia*, 12: "The Eucharist . . . applies to men and women today the reconciliation won once for all by Christ for mankind in every age. 'The sacrifice of Christ and the sacrifice of the Eucharist are *one single sacrifice*' " (emphasis in the original, quoting *Catechism of the Catholic Church*, 1367, which in turn refers to Trent's decree on the sacrifice of the Mass, ch. 2 [DH §1743]).

58. On this point the Council of Trent, in a passage later frequently recalled, crystallizes what had already been Thomas's own teaching: "Una enim eademque est hostia, idem nunc offerens sacerdotum ministerio, qui se ipsum tunc in cruce obtulit, sola offerendi ratione diversa" (DH §1743).

59. For a reading of Thomas congruent with these last remarks, together with suggestive arguments on how to deal with the problem of past and present in the Eucharistic sacrifice (based on the unique ontology of the hypostatic union), see de La Soujeole, "La présence dans les saints mystères."

Chapter 5

Christian Satisfaction and Sacramental Reconciliation

Romanus Cessario, OP

By divine condescension, human reality has been created in order to enter into communion with the fellowship of the divine persons.[1] This destiny, moreover, remains strictly supernatural. The open-endedness of the human intellect and of human love remains as it were the negative condition for the achievement of this supernatural destiny. In addition, this basically human structure aptitudinally images the personal communion of the Father, the Son, and the Holy Spirit in knowledge and love. The gracious conferral of resources proportionate to a supernatural destiny of communion complement and fulfill what remains only a trajectory impressed upon human nature. First of all, habitual grace transforms the human person so as to share in the divine nature and, then, the theological virtues confer a share in the very divine loving and knowing. Thus, the merely aptitudinal imaging of the three divine persons coincident with human nature itself is achieved as an actual imaging of the three divine persons regarding both their communion in the divine nature and their personal communion in knowledge and love. It should be noted, then, that the image of the three divine persons, the created analogue of perichoresis, remains actualized in precisely those dimensions of consciousness as free self-determination through love that also consti-tutes the ratio of human historicity. In this saving action, the imma-nent and visible mysteries of the incarnate Son both reveal and point

---

1. This chapter previously appeared in *Communio* 16 (1989): 186–96. Reprinted with permission of the author.

to the invisible transcendence of the Trinity, fulfilling Christ's intention to turn everything over to the Father. "For he must reign until he has put all his enemies under his feet" (1 Corinthians 15:25).

In Saint Thomas's view, a particular expression of divine love and justice is showing mercy. Indeed, it is this condescension that accounts for the Incarnation and actively shapes all that transpires in the human intellect and will of Christ. To the human will of Christ, God communicates the fullness of supernatural love as a capital endowment, such that his love for the Father should be both abounding love for us and the love of the Father on behalf of the members of his Body. Thus rectified by charity, the human will of Christ fulfills the divine justice; that is, performs the substance of Adam's original establishment in justice: a complete submission and subjection of all human energies and interest to the Father. It is this "evangelical" justice, suffused by excelling charity, that forms the inner core of Christ's salvific work under its satisfactory aspects. For, in this attitude of subjection and obedience, Christ ratifies the Father's salvific plan within the ambit of his human history and destiny. What remains salvifically determinative and therefore satisfactory about Christ's human destiny therefore is not simply the physical event of his Passion, the exaction of a penalty of death, but the interior attitudes of love, obedience, and self-disposal in the Father's favor that animate Christ's sufferings. The perfect interplay of the Father's loving initiative to save humankind and of Christ's human response remains a crucial feature of Christ's satisfactory work, according to Saint Thomas, for that communion of love restores our own imaging communion with the Trinity.

On the positive side, however, the impulse to identify the atonement as an integral and connected part of the trinitarian movement in the world did contribute toward the solution of one prob
lem intrinsic to the theology of satisfaction. How can a past historical event, such as the death of Christ, remain effective for salvation in every subsequent historical moment? Theologians still wrestle with accounts given to support the universal character of Christian redemption. Even so, it is interesting to note the theological intuition of the medieval theologians. Because they generally held to the authentic transcendence of God, these theologians, by representing the sacrifice of Christ as really involved with the Trinity, provided a way out of a

problem which later theologians, either less convinced of the divine transcendence or, from a methodological perspective, more intent on remaining strictly within the limits of historical and textual analysis, still find difficult to resolve. Indeed, fundamental to an adequate sacramental theology remains an account that explains how the actions of the divine and human agents converge in the achievement of the sacramental effects. In Christ, of course, the hypostatic union provides both the explanatory concept for the Incarnation and the model for all other mediations in the Church. But the sacraments, since they involve individual human agency in both the minister and the recipient—"separated instruments," in the phrase of Aquinas— require further explanation. Among other purposes, then, in this chapter I will advance a proposal about how one can coherently affirm this "double agency" in sacramental theory.

Of course, Saint Thomas's account of Christ's salvific work in its satisfactory character addresses not merely the achievement of this sort of personal communion between head and members and of the whole body through its head with triune fellowship. It equally confronts the historical situation of such communion and that which has rendered such communion historically impossible: the reality of human sin, historical sin as a concrete determinant of universal human history. The "economy" of sin is by no means either ultimate or even equiparent with the economy of salvation in the Christian view. Indeed, inasmuch as human moral failure instantiates whatever lacks due order, characterized by deficient causality and unintelligibility, its historical shape remains parasitic upon God's governance of his creation.

If it be adequate to interpret the authentic tradition, theological anthropology must embrace a fully Christian view of man. This, moreover, requires a broad view of creation, providence, and sin. Creation remains a coming forth from God's sustaining power and providence. And whatever the full meaning of fallen nature entails, it surely includes certain privative effects in the powers of the soul, the intellect, the will, and the sense appetites; these amount, in effect, to a disordering of the powers of the soul among themselves. As something concrete and consonant with the biblical teaching, the alienation accomplished by original sin exists on three distinct levels: the individual, societal, and the divine. Thus, in our post-lapsarian state, deprived of the special endowments that our first parents enjoyed, the work of Christian grace on fallen nature must always remain elevating and restorative, or as the scholastics put it, *gratia sanans et elevans.* And this points up the constitutional dyads of redemption: satisfaction and merit, image-restoration and image-perfection. In fact, we could summarize the discussion in this way. A good Christian anthropology achieves a balance between the Scylla embodied in rationalist accounts of original sin with their correlative reductionist view of Christ's work and the Charybdis instantiated in pessimistic descriptions of human nature with their implied deficient trust in Christ's efficacy. As the Fathers remind us, Christ has become our integrity.

The sacrament of Penance holds a special place in the sacramental life of the Church. Pope John Paul II, for example, points to this sacrament as a principal locus where through the working of the Holy Spirit the human person encounters the reconciliation effected by Christ's salvific death.[2] As happens in every sacrament, Penance also manifests God's saving providence for the baptized member of Christ's Body or, as Saint Leo the Great remarks, "Our Redeemer's presence has passed into the sacraments."[3] In the case of Penance, however, this providential care exists in order to provide for a certain contingency in human affairs. In short, we require Penance as a remedy for sins committed after Baptism. This explains why the Council of Trent accepted the metaphorical reference, a second plank after shipwreck, as an apt image for this sacrament.[4] Expressing one of his fundamental convictions about this sacrament, John Paul II writes, saying that "for a Christian, the sacrament of Penance is the ordinary way of obtaining forgiveness and the remission of serious sins committed after baptism."[5] The sacrament of Penance, then, provides the sinner with an opportunity to encounter personally the cause of divine reconciliation.

Following a principle basic to and constitutive of every sacramental reality, theologians advance the view that the efficacy

---

2. See John Paul II, "Post-Synodal Apostolic Exhortation on Reconciliation and Penance in the Mission of the Church Today" (1984). Cf. *Origins* 14: 433–58.

3. Sermon 2 *On the Ascension,* c. 11 (PL LIV: 398).

4. "Si quis . . . paenitentiam non recte 'secundum post naufragium tabulam' apellari: an s." (DS §1702).

5. *Reconciliatio et paenitentia,* 31.I.

of Penance derives from the Passion of Christ itself. Only the satisfaction of Christ can merit our spiritual well-being. But Penance holds a secondary place relative to the integrity, which the other sacraments, especially Baptism and the Eucharist, confer and preserve on the member of Christ's Body. Hence the Church correctly, if only metaphorically, refers to the sacrament as "the second plank after shipwreck." Indeed, the first protection for those crossing a sea remains the safety provided by an intact ship; but after shipwreck, one can only cling to a plank as a second remedy. Thus Aquinas concludes: "So also, the first protection in the sea of this life remains that a person preserve spiritual integrity; but if one, by committing sin, should lose it, the second remedy is that regained through penance."[6] However obliquely, this emphasis on the conditional character of Penance points to the mystery of human freedom and divine providence. The sacrament of Penance, then, establishes the condition necessary to transform sin into a *felix culpa*.

The history of this sacrament within the Church evidences several misconceptions concerning its nature and efficacy. To begin with one example of misguided instruction on how the Christian should react to sin and temptation, historical Quietism subverted the Church's teaching in order to accommodate a spirituality that was negligent with respect to moral discipline. And although current interest in the works of Madame Guyon suggests a limited renaissance of this view, the ecclesiastical condemnation and subsequent punishment of Miguel Molinos still remains an effective witness to the truth that the simplicity of God's love never provides an excuse for vicious behavior.[7] Likewise, the sacrament of Christ's reconciliation can never become an excuse for moral indifference or spiritual laxity. Mortal sin remains the greatest evil that can befall the human person. Indeed, spiritual authors continually warn against the especially vicious sin of ingratitude for the forgiveness of past sins. To be sure, mortal sin always embodies the prime analogue for any sinful activity, because only this kind of aversion from God destroys the bond of charity and friendship with God which baptismal grace establishes in the soul. So theories about Penance err both by excess and by defect.

---

6. *Summa Theologiae* III, q. 84, a. 6.

7. For example, between 1975 and 1985 Christian Books, Gardiner, ME, published several revised English translations of Madame Guyon's treatises as works of popular piety.

We need to understand, then, how Penance works. When
the medieval theologians sought to explain the constitutive reality
of a given sacrament, they identified three principal elements present
in each of the *sacra septenaria*: 1) the liturgical rite itself; 2) the interior
effect or personal grace which the sacrament accomplishes; and
3) the permanent feature or abiding aspect of the sacrament. In the
technical language of the schools, we refer to these respectively as the
sacramentum tantum, the *res tantum*, and the *res et sacramentum*.[8] Since
the grace of Penance remains especially allied with the satisfaction
of Christ, we can freely assign the work of image-restoration and
image-perfection as the principal interior effect of Penance. Again,
leaving the matter of the liturgical rite aside for the moment, we
can inquire about the permanent feature that Penance sacramentally
establishes within the Church. In other terms, how does this sacrament mediate the Passion of Christ to those whom the Holy Spirit
draws toward the tribunal of God's mercy?

This question, in fact, exacerbated certain medieval theologians who found it difficult to pin down in a theological formulation
something contingent like personal sorrow. Even Aquinas's position
on the sacramentality of Penance remains a difficult feature of his
entire sacramental theology. After considering the relative merits of
other views, he mentions the *res et sacramentum*, the abiding sacrament
of Penance, as the penitent's sorrow for sin based on faith in the
saving power of Christ's mysteries. Already inspired by the gift of
the Spirit, the repentant sinner's renewed love for God combines
with the action of the priest's absolution to bring the penitent toward
a renewed sense of belonging to God. Thus, the phrase of Saint
Augustine serves to remind us of the cooperative character of this
sacrament: "He who has created you without yourself will not justify
you without yourself."[9] Modern theologians, on the other hand,
prefer to speak simply of solemn admission to the Eucharist, thereby
setting aside the difficult questions involved in stabilizing personal

---

8. Contemporary sacramental theology, with its emphasis on the symbolic and
anthropological aspects of the sacraments, usually does not feature these distinctions. But see
Colman E. O'Neill, *Sacramental Realism. A General Theory of the Sacraments* (Wilmington, DE:
Michael Glazier, Inc. 1983), esp. 98, 106, 171 ff., 181 ff. Republished (Chicago: Midwest
Theological Forum, 1998).

9. Ibid., 175–7 for a brief discussion of Aquinas's position on the sacramentality of
Penance.

contrition within the ambit of sacramental efficacy and ecclesial communion.

The tradition enumerates three principal elements which compose the sacrament of Penance: contrition of the heart, confession of the lips, and the satisfaction of works. John Paul II includes reference to these "realities or parts" in *Reconciliatio et paenitentia.* "Satisfaction," he writes, "is the final act which crowns the sacramental sign of Penance."[10] He goes on to explain that acts of satisfaction, in addition to joining the sinner's own physical and spiritual mortification to the Passion of Jesus Christ, remain valuable signs of the personal commitment which the Christian has made to God in the sacrament to begin a new life. The imposition of an individual satisfaction, then, remains integral to the celebration of Reconciliation as a sacrament. It acts in the same way that true sorrow and (under normal circumstances) particular confession of sins also do. The penance, as custom refers to it, both completes the necessary elements of sacramental Reconciliation and moves the forgiven sinner toward a renewed life of virtue and charity within the Church. Furthermore, everything that Christ accomplished by his satisfaction now stands at the disposal of the newly reconciled member of his Body.

This explains Aquinas's contention that in Penance not only is the restoration of the balance of justice sought, as in retributive justice, but above all the reconciliation of friendship.[11] The very notion of commutative justice prevails even here, resembling that which can exist even between members of a family. When, for example, a father distributes benefits to his children, he does so according to a wisdom and love which he alone possesses. This allusion remains the controlling image in Aquinas's explanation of Reconciliation. In fact, the actual living out of image-restorative works, now ratified by the sacrament of Christ's love, itself constitutes the achievement of divine grace. The liturgy still reflects this theology of satisfaction when it counsels priests to join the following prayer after the sacramental absolution: "May the Passion of Our Lord Jesus Christ, the merits of the blessed Virgin Mary and of all the saints, and also whatever good

---

10. *Reconciliatio et paenitentia*, 31.III.

11. Aquinas actually makes this point in the context of the virtue of penitence: "And it is thus that the penitent turns to God, with the purpose of amendment as a servant to his master, . . . and as the son to his father, . . . and as a wife to her husband." III, q. 85, a. 3.

you do and evil you endure, be cause for the remission of your sins, the increase of grace, and the reward of life everlasting."[12] Through it, the Church, making explicit reference to the *thesaurus ecclesiae*, as the merits of Christ and of the saints over which she holds definitive authority are called, sacramentalizes the whole life of the believer. It also signifies the reviviscence of grace.

To be sure, the institute of frequent confession does not occupy a central place in contemporary pastoral theology, and we find very little written today which urges the celebration of the sacrament precisely as a means toward spiritual growth. But John Paul II still maintains that "the frequent use of the sacrament [of Penance] . . . strengthens the awareness that even minor sins offend God and harm the Church, the Body of Christ."[13] Christian satisfaction and the sacrament of Penance, which establishes it as an effective means for image-perfection, both accomplish this goal and at the same time bring Christ's mission to completion. Saint John tells us that "in this is love perfected with us, that we may have confidence for the day of judgment, because as he is so are we in this world" (1 John 4:12). Indeed, Christ wants to fulfill this mission, which he has received from the Father: "The glory which thou hast given me I have given to them, that they may be one even as we are one, I in them and thou in me, that they may become perfectly one, so that the world may know that thou hast sent me and hast loved me" (John 17:24). The reconciliation of a fallen race remains Christ's glory, the very task given him by the Father to accomplish.

We read in Saint Luke's Gospel account, "Father I have sinned against heaven and before you" (Luke 5:11–32). The power of Christ's Passion mediated in the sacrament turns the penitent person back to God, with a purpose of amendment, as a son and daughter turn toward their father. It is precisely in this aspect of divine forgiveness, that the Church especially discerns the healing or medicinal character of Reconciliation. "And this is linked to the fact," writes John Paul II, "that the Gospel frequently presents Christ as healer, while

---

12. *Ordo Paenitentiae*, no. 93.

13. *Reconciliatio et paenitentia*, 32. In our day, Adrienne von Speyr stresses this important practice in the spiritual life. See her *Confession*, trans. Douglas W. Scott (San Francisco: Ignatius Press, 1985).

his redemptive work is often called medicina salutis."[14] Further, if we look at this from the perspective of the divine action operative in the sacrament, we can recognize unequivocally the divine intention that Christ manifests, what Saint John refers to as his glory. Christ comes to fulfill a task, which is to reveal God's true purposes concerning our salvation. Christ manifests what lies within the heart of the Father: "Father, they are your gift to me. I wish that where I am they also may be with me, that they may see my glory that you gave me, because you loved me before the foundation of the world" (John 17: 24). Above all, and like a human father, God desires more to draw his prodigal children back to loving union with himself than to punish them according to the canons of vindicative justice. And our awareness of this desire should consequently move us toward seeking the sacrament with greater and greater frequency and fervor.

Foremost in any theological discussion remain two mysteries, the Incarnation and the Trinity, a fact which all Catholic theologians accept. When practiced in accord with their original purposes, Christian soteriology and sacramental theory lead us to a personal communion with the three-personed God. That remains the only goal indicating where the work of Christ leads. Theologians speak about the missions of the divine persons as a way of indicating the active role that God takes in our personal histories. The missions, in turn, reflect the trinitarian processions that, with all of their inner necessity in knowledge and love, constitute the very Godhead itself. These trinitarian missions, moreover, form special relationships in those to whom God freely extends justification in the Church of faith and sacraments. Indeed, the visible sending of the Son and invisible coming of the Holy Spirit comprise the principal trinitarian missions that characterize the economy of salvation.[15]

The patristic doctrine of *perichoresis*, *circuminsessio* in Latin, reminds us of the fundamental unity and consubstantiality of the divine persons. But what the Latin theologians further distinguish as *circumincessio* points to another aspect of God's inner life; namely, the attraction which the divine persons exercise upon one another,

---

14. *Reconciliatio et paenitentia*, 31.III.

15. For an expert discussion of the trinitarian implications latent in sacramental Reconciliation, see William J. Hill, OP, *The Three Personed God: The Trinity as a Mystery of Salvation* (Washington, DC: The Catholic University of America Press, 1982), esp. 273–314.

drawing together all those parts of the divine plan known only to God. Accordingly, on a personal level, the blessed Trinity remains present to the souls of the justified believer as "object known and loved." Although this formulation reflects the realist preference for the primacy of knowledge in the human person, the formulation nonetheless makes a clear reference to the unity of human subjectivity. Indeed, the spiritual tradition prefers to call this knowledge quasi-experiential in order to emphasize the importance of the non-cognitive elements that mark it as unique. Like the gifts of the Holy Spirit, which constitute the special and privileged endowments of the Christian believer, the three-personed God remains the principal and unique source of spiritual benefit and growth for the members of Christ's Body. So the sacraments point to God. And in the sacrament of Penance, especially, we discover how the Trinity effects a sacrament of salvation for those who remain united with the incarnate Son.

Furthermore, medicinal punishment as an effect of human moral fault shows that God's loving intentions retain the upper hand in guiding human history to its true destiny. It is radically the Incarnation of the Word and Christ's consequent disposal of his historical freedom in loving response to the Father which show that what remains uppermost and triumphant remains the Father's love. In that perfect response to the Father's saving will, Christ has freely and lovingly chosen solidarity with human history and a history of suffering (imposed as a punishment). In virtue of Christ's solidarity with suffering humanity, penal suffering becomes "once and for all" truly restorative and rectifies human willing. For, in truth, Christ "learned obedience through suffering," inasmuch as the full range of Christ's subjection of himself to the Father's saving will includes the acceptance of suffering experienced as the historical locus for obedient and loving acceptance of that will. The supernatural gifts that the body derive from their head accordingly effect a personal solidarity with him in other situations of human suffering. The grace and charity that Christ's members receive from him and in him always remain the grace and love of his Passion. These conform Christ's Body to Christ's own obedience and love. This conformity urges the members of the Church to "make up what is lacking in the sufferings of Christ"—that is, to supply their own free ratification of the experience of the cross as the definitive historical shape of communion

with the Father and the Holy Spirit in and through their Head.
Union in and with the mind of Christ enables Christians to transform
and shape human history by extending Christ's salvific work through
culture and society. This openness, in short, helps us "to redeem
the time."

Chapter 6

Saint Thomas Aquinas on the Anointing of the Sick (Extreme Unction)

John F. Boyle

Editor's note:
The name "extreme unction" comes directly from the Latin, *unctio extrema*, meaning "final anointing." This was the common name for the sacrament known after the second Vatican Council as "the Anointing of the Sick." The change in name reflects an emphasis precisely on the pastoral needs of the sick (see *Catechism of the Catholic Church* [CCC], 1499–1532). While the Church now speaks of grave illness, Saint Thomas stressed illness at the point of death. Of course, the distinction between grave illness and the threat of death was perhaps at best theoretical in a pre-industrial world. The essential features of the sacrament theologically considered, however, have not changed. The CCC lists as the effects of the sacrament: "the uniting of the sick person to the passion of Christ, for his own good and that of the whole Church; the strengthening, peace, and courage to endure in a Christian manner the sufferings of illness or old age; the forgiveness of sins, if the person was not able to obtain it through the sacrament of penance; the restoration of health, if it is conducive to the salvation of his soul; the preparation for passing over to eternal life" (CCC, 1532). As Professor Boyle shows, these basic elements, in the CCC simply in list form, are those of Saint Thomas; the task Saint Thomas sets himself is to establish a fitting and coherent speculative order among these elements. In this, his contribution to the theology of the Anointing of the Sick is of enduring influence. In this chapter, Professor Boyle uses the name "Extreme Unction" when describing the sacrament as Saint Thomas and his contemporaries knew it and wrote about it.

Thomas Aquinas has little to say about the Anointing of the Sick (*extrema unctio*), at least in comparison with the other sacraments. In fact, his contemporary scholastics have little to say about Extreme Unction. Even with little to say, they still manage to disagree.

They all agree, however, upon certain features of Extreme Unction, beginning with the affirmation that it is a sacrament. It has to do with healing. This means spiritual healing can, uniquely among the sacraments, also include healing of the body. Insofar as it has to do with spiritual healing, it has something to do with spiritual sickness, that is, sin and its effects. Finally, it is a sacrament for those physically sick, specifically for those whose illness is of sufficient gravity as to threaten death. All of these elements are found in Peter Lombard's *Book of Sentences*,[1] and on them there is agreement.

With his usual caginess, Lombard offers no speculative ordering among these elements. And so the scholastics are left with the question: How to conceive of their ordering and integrity in such a way as to articulate what is distinctive about this particular sacrament? On this question there is rather more disagreement among the scholastics; in the thirteenth century there was thinking yet to be done about Extreme Unction. With regard to the principal fault lines among the scholastic theologians—whether it is ordered to the forgiveness of venial sin and whether it was instituted by Christ himself—Thomas's position remains constant throughout his career (no to the former, yes to the latter). Nonetheless, in the effort to provide a coherent articulation of the sacrament, Thomas's thought shifts in the course of his career; it is the task of this chapter to chart this development in his thought.

The first, and by far the lengthiest, of Saint Thomas's treatments of Extreme Unction is found in his commentary on distinction 23 of the fourth book of Peter Lombard's *Book of Sentences*.[2]

The opening of the *divisio textus* gives the analogical frame for Thomas's analysis.

> After the Master has determined about baptism, which is the sacrament for those entering, and about confirmation, eucharist and penance which are the sacraments for those progressing, here, in the fifth place, he determines concerning extreme unction which is the sacrament of those departing.[3]

1. The treatment of Extreme Unction is found in book IV, distinction 23; see Peter Lombard, *Sententiae in IV libris distinctae*, 3rd ed. (Grottaferrata: Editiones Collegii S. Bonaventurae, 1971–1981), vol. 2, pp. 390–3.

2. Thomas Aquinas, *Scriptum super Sententiis*, vol. 4, ed. M. F. Moos (Paris: Lethielleux, 1947) has only the commentary on book IV through distinction 22. For distinction 23, see Thomas Aquinas, *Opera omnia* (Parma: Typis Petri Fiaccadori, 1858), tom. VII, vol. 2, pp. 873–83.

3. *Sup. IV Sent.* 23.divisio textus (873a). See also *Sup. IV Sent.* 2.1.2.resp. (Moos, 82–3) where this is one of the ways used to account for the number of sacraments. These five are put

The analogy is founded on life's movement: entrance, progress, departure. Within this frame, Extreme Unction is the sacrament of departure. By way of this analogy, Thomas neatly distinguishes Extreme Unction from the other six sacraments.

But what does this sacrament do for the departing? To what is it ordered? To answer this, Thomas turns first to its signification. The sign, the *sacramentum*, in Extreme Unction is the anointing, which Thomas, in union with the tradition, takes to be medicinal.[4] Thus, Extreme Unction is a spiritual medicine, signified by medicinal bodily anointing. If it is medicine, then there must be an illness; spiritual illness is sin and its effects, and thus it would follow that Extreme Unction as medicine is ordered to the healing of sin. But this raises a question: How does Extreme Unction differ from Baptism and Penance, both of which also directly heal man of sin?[5] Thomas distinguishes these according to three different analogies: Baptism brings about new life, Penance raises from the dead, Extreme Unction heals the sick. In distinguishing Penance and Extreme Unction, Thomas says that Penance is ordered to the resuscitation of the spiritually dead, while Extreme Unction is ordered to the healing of the spiritually living but sick.

If Baptism forgives original and mortal sin, and Penance forgives postbaptismal mortal sin, does this then mean that Extreme Unction is ordered to the forgiveness of venial sin? No. Penance is properly ordered to the forgiveness of sin; there is no need for a further sacrament directly ordered to forgiving sins, including venial sins, which, in fact, are forgiven by any increase in grace and devotion. So precisely to what is the medicine of Extreme Unction ordered? It is ordered to the remains of sin, the *reliquiae peccati,* which Saint Thomas here describes as a weakness of mind that remains after the forgiveness of sins. But would it not seem that everyone is ever in

---

together insofar as they pertain to the remedial good of one person; Holy Orders and Matrimony are sacraments ordered to the remedial good of the whole church, not of one person.

4. *Sup. IV Sent.* 23.1.2.1.sol. (876a) for all of what follows from the commentary on the *Sentences* unless otherwise noted.

5. In the *Sentences* commentary, Thomas says that the effect intended in all seven sacraments is the healing of the sickness of sin (see *Sup. IV Sent.* 23.1.1.sol. [874a]). Thus, while the specification of Extreme Unction as medicine in relation to Baptism and Penance is Thomas's principal focus, it is at least implicitly within a larger context of specification with regard to all the other sacraments.

need of such a sacrament? To specify those who are to receive this sacrament, Thomas returns to the analogical frame according to which this sacrament is the sacrament of those departing. Because the soul is preparing for its immanent departure, it most especially needs to attend to those remains of sin that have served to weaken it and render it less than fit for glory. And so it is that this sacrament is not given against those defects by which the spiritual life is simply removed, namely original and mortal sin, but against those defects by which a man is spiritually weakened such that he has not the perfect vigor requisite for the acts of a life of grace and glory.

Thomas's analysis of Extreme Unction in his commentary on the *Sentences* rests upon two of the agreed upon elements of the sacrament. The medicinal *sacramentum* distinguishes it from the other sacraments, most notably the resuscitating sacrament of Penance; its reservation to the sick in danger of death specifies it as the sacrament for the departing within the broader analogical frame of life's movement.

The remaining two elements follow from the medicinal *sacramentum*. The sacrament may heal the body as well as the soul, provided it serves the spiritual good of the soul.[6] That it is to be administered only to the sick is a requirement of the signification of the sacrament: corporeal medicine for the physically sick signifying spiritual medicine for the spiritually sick.[7]

With the *Summa Contra Gentiles*, the analogical frame has changed and with it the analysis of Extreme Unction. The analogy for the sacraments is the one familiar to students of Saint Thomas; that of spiritual life conforming to corporeal life. The specifics of corporeal life serve as the analogues for distinguishing the sacraments: generation, growth, nourishment, and so forth.[8]

The analogy from the movement of life is now gone, replaced by a more precise and substantial analogy. The weakness of the analogy from movement of life is best seen in the Anointing of the Sick itself. If Baptism is entrance, and if Confirmation, Eucharist, Penance, and Reconciliation are progress, then precisely from what is

---

6. *Sup. IV Sent.* 23.1.2.2.sol. (876b).

7. *Sup. IV Sent.* 23.2.2.1.sol. (881a).

8. Thomas Aquinas, *Summa Contra Gentiles* (SC6), bk. IV, ch. 58, in *Opera omnia*, ed. Fratres Praedicatores (Rome: Apud sedem commisionis leoninae, 1930), tom. XV, pp. 193–4.

the Anointing of the Sick a departure? From the spiritual life one entered into in Baptism and progressed in through Confirmation, Eucharist, Penance, and Reconciliation? Surely not. But if it is merely departure from corporeal life, then there is no analogy from the corporeal to the spiritual in the case of the Anointing of the Sick; it is merely univocal death. One could no doubt save the analogy, but the effort would rather contort it.

With departure now gone, where does the Anointing of the Sick stand in the new analogical frame?[9] In corporeal life, we find not only birth, growth, and sustenance, but also illness; and for illness we need medicine. So it is, too, in the spiritual life. The Anointing of the Sick is spiritual medicine. The simple beauty of this development permits Thomas to unite the healing signified by the *sacramentum* of Extreme Unction with its place in the over-arching analogical frame of the sacraments. What was two in the commentary on the *Sentences*—healing and departure—is now simply one: healing.

In the *Summa Contra Gentiles*, however, there is another medicine in addition to Extreme Unction: Penance. Penance is no longer some kind of resuscitation of the dead as in the *Sentences* commentary. But if Penance is a kind of medicine, how is it to be distinguished from Extreme Unction? The answer is a tidy one: Penance is spiritual medicine; Extreme Unction is both spiritual and corporeal medicine. Thus Thomas keeps the essential signification of medicine now expressed in the analogical frame, but also links it directly to the corporeal healing of the sacrament.

The spiritual and pastoral reality of Thomas's keen hylomorphism is manifestly at work here. He says that some sin directly affects the health of the body. Conversely, while bodily illness may be an occasion of spiritual good, as a form of satisfaction for sins, for example, such illness may also impede spiritual health as when the weakness of the body impedes the exercise of the virtues. Because therefore the body ought to be properly disposed to the soul, it is only fitting that there be a spiritual medicine directed to corporeal illness as it arises from sin. Thus Thomas specifies Extreme Unction as the sacrament that is ordered against the weakness of the body insofar as it arises from sin.

---

9. The treatment of Extreme Unction is found in SCG, bk. IV, ch. 73 (233–4).

Still, the sacrament may not, in fact, heal the body. This does not mean that it is useless, for the Anointing of the Sick is also ordered against other consequences of sin (*sequelae peccati*), which are the inclination to evil and the difficulty of pursuing the good. This follows because weaknesses of the soul are closer to sin than weaknesses of the body; thus, if the Anointing of the Sick is ordered to the latter, then all the more so to the former.

But this returns us to the question of how to distinguish the Anointing of the Sick from Penance and Reconciliation. After all, spiritual weaknesses are healed through penance insofar as the penitent is drawn away from evil and inclined toward good through the works of virtue he employs in satisfying for his sins. Here Thomas appeals to a reality of the spiritual life. The fact is that man does not attend to such weaknesses as he should in Penance and Reconciliation whether through negligence, the many occupations of life, the lack of time, or other such reasons. The Anointing of the Sick has, therefore, been provided for humanity such that the healing begun in Penance and Reconciliation might be completed and that humanity might be freed from temporal punishments due to sin. And all of this is ordered to this end: that nothing should remain in man that might impede the soul in coming to perceive the glory of God upon leaving the body. With this immediate ordering to preparation for death, Thomas explains that the sacrament also forgives sins, for it happens that a man has neither knowledge nor recollection of all the sins committed since this present life cannot be lived without its daily sins.

The analysis of Extreme Unction in the *Summa Contra Gentiles* is tighter than that in the *Sentences* commentary because Thomas has united the *sacramentum* of Extreme Unction as medicine with the frame of the analogy from corporeal life. The medicinal is defining. In distinguishing it from Penance, he specifies it according to its twofold spiritual and corporeal healing. From the healing of bodily illness as an effect of sin, Thomas can move readily enough to the healing of spiritual weaknesses that are effects of sin. Thus, it is a healing of the remains of sin. This is characterized as a kind of completion of the sacrament of Penance. At this point he introduces the specification of preparation for death and hence the immediate need of that completion apart from the effects of Penance. In concluding his chapter on Extreme Unction, Thomas speaks of the sacrament as a consummation of all the sacraments.

That it is reserved for the physically sick is again a matter of preserving the full signification of the sacrament.

This same analysis is present in the little work *De articulis fidei et sacramentis ecclesiae.*[10]

When we come to the *Summa Theologiae*, however, Thomas shifts again. Of course, Thomas stopped writing the *tertia pars* before he got to Extreme Unction, and so we must go by the few remarks he makes in considering the seven sacraments as a whole, not knowing precisely how the details of Extreme Unction would have been ultimately presented.[11]

The same analogical frame of spiritual life conformed to corporeal life is present and definitive. Both Penance and Reconciliation and the Anointing of the Sick are medicines. This remains unchanged. But Thomas has reconsidered the relationship between these two medicines. The specification of the *Summa Contra Gentiles* by which Penance was ordered to spiritual health and Extreme Unction to both spiritual and corporeal health is gone, replaced by a new distinction between health and robustness of health. In physical life we distinguish between health and robustness of health. One might be without illness and in this sense healthy, but lack the robustness of health that comes from exercise and a good diet. The spectrum of health beyond simply not being sick is a reality of corporeal life that Saint Thomas now applies to the spiritual life. Thus Penance and Reconciliation is ordered to spiritual health in that it is the medicine against the illness of sin and thereby restores spiritual health. The Anointing of the Sick is ordered to robustness of spiritual life; it is the medicine that attends to the various remains of sin that weaken or limit a healthy but not vigorous spiritual life. The distinction is present in the earlier writings, but here it takes on speculative purpose. Its value lies in being a distinction that is truer to the analogy of bodily and spiritual life. While the *Summa Contra Gentiles* has the analogy from bodily illness to spiritual illness, the introduction of bodily illness itself into the specification of spiritual illness is analogically awkward. It is, of

---

10. See Thomas Aquinas, *De articulis fidei et ecclesiae sacramentis*, II, in *Opera omnia*, ed. Fratres Praedicatores (Rome: Editori di San Tommaso, 1979), tom. XLII, pp. 252–3, 256, 257.

11. *Summa Theologiae* III, q. 65, a. 1.

course, not insurmountable, and one could certainly say that it reflects the hylomorphic reality of man, so prominent in the account of the *Summa Contra Gentiles*. Still, Thomas shifts the analogy here and, as usual, does so without notice or explanation. The result is a cleaner analogy.

In this refined analogy by which the Anointing of the Sick is medicine for robust and vigorous spiritual health, it is ordered to the remains of sin (the *reliquiae peccati* again). Precisely how Saint Thomas would play this out, we can only surmise, a task I am not inclined to undertake. But the change itself is speculatively helpful. In the *Summa Contra Gentiles*, Thomas used one *reliquia* of sin, bodily illness, to specify the sacrament in relation to Penance, and then by a kind of *a fortiori* argument moved from the species (corporeal illness) to the genus (*reliquiae peccati*). In the *Summa Theologiae*, the remains of sin themselves can simply be the defining object within the analogical frame of robustness of health. Corporeal health will now follow neatly insofar as it is a harmful effect of sin. Because it is not needed to specify the medicinal quality of Extreme Unction, it can take a more fittingly ordered place as one of the remains of sin, which themselves precisely as remains now specify that medicinal quality. Even though we lack Saint Thomas's full treatment of Extreme Unction in the *Summa Theologiae*, we nonetheless find, in what we do have, a tighter and more unified account of the sacrament than found in his earlier work.

What Saint Thomas has to say about Extreme Unction is, all said and done, a rather modest corner of his thinking on the sacraments. Perhaps because of its very modesty, one cannot help but be struck by the attention he gives it in the delicate refinements of his thinking. What we see especially in his treatment of Extreme Unction is an ever more attentive reflection on its medicinal reality. The emergence of the analogical frame for the sacraments of spiritual life conformed to corporeal life recasts the sacrament and simultaneously gives a new unity to the treatment. From then on an increasingly clear and precise analysis of the primary analog of corporeal health makes for an increasingly clear distinction between Penance and Reconciliation and the Anointing of the Sick. It is precisely the clarification of the primary analogs from corporeal reality that makes possible the increasing speculative unity of Thomas's treatment of

Extreme Unction. We see how Thomas's attention, indeed his fidelity, to the primary analogs helps us understand all the better the hidden graces of God.

Chapter 7

Holy Orders and Ecclesial Hierarchy in Aquinas

Matthew Levering

The *Catechism of the Catholic Church* (CCC) observes that "the sacrament of Holy Orders communicates a 'sacred power' which is none other than that of Christ. The exercise of this authority must therefore be measured against the model of Christ, who by love made himself the least and the servant of all" (CCC 1551). Likewise, the Catechism states, "The ministerial priesthood has the task not only of representing Christ—Head of the Church—before the assembly of the faithful, but also of acting in the name of the whole Church when presenting to God the prayer of the Church, and above all when offering the Eucharistic sacrifice" (CCC 1552). Yet, in a community that Christ willed to be characterized by profound humility and mutual self-subordination (cf. Mark 9:35, 10:43–45), should some Christians have hierarchical authority vis-à-vis other Christians? Furthermore, why should only priests consecrate the Eucharist, which Saint Paul envisions as the sign of Christian unity: "Because there is one bread, we who are many are one body, for we all partake of the one bread" (1 Corinthians 10:17)? As we will see, issues such as these stand at the heart of Thomas Aquinas's theology of Holy Orders. I will first draw upon his discussion of orders in his *Sentences* commentary, and second turn to his discussion of orders in the *Summa Contra Gentiles*.

ORDERS IN THE *COMMENTARY ON THE SENTENCES:* SUPPLEMENT TO THE *SUMMA THEOLOGIAE*

When Thomas Aquinas's friend and scribe, Reginald of Piperno, completed the *Summa Theologiae* shortly after Aquinas's death, Reginald drew the treatment of the sacrament of Holy Orders from the *Commentary on the Sentences*.[1] The discussion of the sacrament of orders found in the *Supplement* begins with three objections that set forth the reasons against hierarchical authority.

The first objection is that "Order requires subjection and preeminence. But subjection seemingly is incompatible with the liberty whereunto we are called by Christ."[2] What kind of "subjection" does Aquinas have in mind here? His language—"subjection" versus Christian "liberty"—recalls Saint Paul's rejoicing in Christian freedom from the power of sin: "There is therefore now no condemnation for those who are in Christ Jesus. For the law of the Spirit of life in Christ Jesus has set me free from the law of sin and death" (Romans 8:1–2). Saint Paul does not reject "subjection" per se. For Paul subjection is the foundation of true freedom, but only so long as it is subjection to God. Paul writes, "But now that you have been set free from sin and have become slaves of God, the return you get is sanctification and its end, eternal life. For the wages of sin is death, but the free gift of God is eternal life in Christ Jesus our Lord" (Romans 6:22–23).

In his answer to the objection, Aquinas makes clear that the objector has in view not subjection to God, but rather political/ economic subjection or slavery. In this context, Aquinas rejects such subjection or slavery as incompatible with the fullness of Christian freedom. He states, "The subjection of slavery is incompatible with liberty; for slavery consists in lording over others and employing them for one's own profit."[3] Is the hierarchical structure of the Church,

---

1. For discussion of Aquinas's treatment of the sacrament of orders in his *Commentary on the Sentences* and its transposition in the *Supplement*, see Pierre-Marie Gy, OP, "Évolution de saint Thomas sur la théologie du sacrament de l'Ordre," *Revue Thomiste* 99 (1999): 181–9. Gy draws upon M. Turrini, "Réginald de Piperno et le texte original de la *Tertia Pars* de la *Somme de théologie* de S. Thomas d'Aquin," *Revue des sciences philosophiques et théologiques* 73 (1989): 233–47.

2. *Summa Theologiae, Suppl.* q. 34, a. 1, obj. 1.

3. Ibid., ad 1.

in which ordinary believers have to receive from and obey bishops/ priests, an instance of the oppressive political corruption whose core is "lording over others"? Aquinas responds that it is not: "Such subjection is not required in Order, whereby those who preside have to seek the salvation of their subjects and not their own profit."[4] Hierarchy in the Church becomes oppressive only when it is understood and used in political and economic terms, as a lever of worldly power and profiteering, rather than in spiritual terms, as an authoritative mission of teaching and sanctifying. Having to be taught and sanctified by bishops/priests is not in itself an instance of anti–Christian subjection.

The second objection against hierarchical order in the Church also probes the question of subjection, this time asking how the subjection of some Christians to other Christians can be compatible with the requirement that *all* Christians subject themselves to all others. Aquinas notes that "he who has received an Order becomes another's superior. But in the Church everyone should deem himself lower than another (Philippians 2:3): *Let each esteem others better than themselves.*"[5] One observes that a bishop or pope receives much attention, admiration, and flattery. Can such a situation truly accord with, or foster the fulfillment of, Paul's injunction in Philippians 2:3? When certain human beings have more power than other human beings, does this not generally lead them to esteem themselves above other human beings, and thereby provide a portal for pride and the oppression of others that results from pride? Aquinas does not deny that pride can follow upon ecclesial office. He notes, however, that office and merit, according to the Christian understanding, are quite different realities. No matter how elevated the office, "Each one should esteem himself lower in merit" than others.[6] Christian charity does not require that everyone possess an office of equal rank, but requires instead a recognition that one's merit is distinct from one's office. Charity, not ecclesial office, is the ground of merit, which is the true "power" in the Church.

If the merit accrued by love is the true power or hierarchy in the Church, however, why have a hierarchy of office? Why not a hierarchy constituted by the witness of love? To use a contemporary

---

4. Ibid.

5. Ibid., obj. 2.

6. Ibid., ad 2.

example, should Mother Teresa have to receive the sacraments from a
priest who is far less meritorious? Indeed, the third objection observes
that among the angels, hierarchy is ordered in precisely this fashion,
that is, in strict accord with merit: "we find Order among the angels
on account of their differing in natural and gratuitous gifts."[7]
Aquinas grants, in the voice of the objector, that angels differ more
clearly in nature—each being its own species—and that the gratuitous gifts of angels are clear to all, whereas "all men are one in
nature, and it is not known who has the higher gifts of grace."[8]
It would appear, then, that a hierarchy ordered by degrees of virtue
is not possible in this life for human beings. The objection concludes that if no hierarchy like the angelic hierarchy is possible, then
there should be no visible hierarchy at all in the Church, built as the
Church is upon charity.

In answering this objection, Aquinas notes that the sacraments of the Church, which hierarchical order in the Church serves,
are not about the holiness of human beings, as if they were anthropo-
centric rites. Rather, the sacraments are about participating in the
holiness of God in Christ Jesus. This has an important consequence
for hierarchical order in the Church: such order depends not upon
degrees of human holiness, but upon efficacious dispensing of the
divine sacraments by which human beings are made holy. Order in
the Church is based ultimately upon the work of Christ and the Spirit
rather than upon the work of mere human beings. It is different
among the angels in heaven, where order "results directly from their
difference in grace" so that "their orders regard their participation of
divine things, and their communicating them in the state of glory."[9]
Among human beings, the situation is the other way around: hierarchical order exists not as the manifestation of diverse creaturely
participations in the grace of the Holy Spirit, but as a means by which
to *enable* creatures to participate in the grace of the Holy Spirit.

For the Church on earth, in short, hierarchical order is not
itself an "order of grace" but a mode of transmitting the grace of the
Holy Spirit sacramentally; it seeks to bring about what the angels
already enjoy in heaven. Aquinas states that "the Orders of the

---

7. Ibid., obj. 3.

8. Ibid.

9. Ibid., ad 3.

Church militant regard the participation in the sacraments and the communication thereof, which are the cause of grace and, in a way, precede grace; and consequently our Orders do not require sanctifying grace, but only the power to dispense the sacraments."[10] Those who imagine the Church's hierarchical order as corresponding "to the difference of sanctifying grace" have misunderstood the instrumental purpose of hierarchical order in the Church.[11]

All three objections, then, probe the basic issue of whether hierarchical power in the Church (Holy Orders) corresponds to and fosters Christian self-subordination to God and neighbor. Ecclesial order is not intended to be for "lording over others" or for imagining that the heavenly hierarchy is based on office rather than on love. Instead, ecclesial order aims at assisting the flourishing of love by means of dispensing the sacraments; ecclesial order finds its (instrumental) purpose, and its limitations, in its sacramental/eucharistic mission. Hierarchical order in the Church is not an end in itself. Yet, as the objections show, Aquinas is well aware of the distortions and abuses that can come with hierarchical order. Why then does God will hierarchical mediation in the Church?

In the *sed contra* and *respondeo*, Aquinas answers that God wills hierarchical mediation in the Church so that creatures might have the dignity of imitating God, of participating in the creator through imitation. This answer seems odd at first glance. God is simple; each divine Person is fully God; there is no higher or lower, better or worse, in God. Why would ecclesial hierarchy constitute, then, an imitation or likeness of God? Following Pseudo-Dionysius, Aquinas observes that hierarchical order imitates God not in God's triune being, but in God's action *ad extra*. To learn to act like God toward all things is to learn to act in accord with a hierarchical pattern. How so? First, Aquinas notes that, "we find order in nature, in that some things are above others, and likewise in glory, as in the angels."[12] God has chosen hierarchy for his creatures. While God could have created a set of creatures perfectly alike in nature and in grace, instead God willed to create an amazingly diverse creation, hierarchically ordered both in nature and in grace. In this way, God

---

10. Ibid.
11. See ibid.
12. Ibid., *sed contra*.

willed that creation express manifold degrees of participation in God's being, wisdom, goodness, beauty, and so forth. Where human beings might have chosen an absolute uniformity among creatures, God wills an extraordinary diversity. In God there must be a delight for particularity and diversity, for the glorious variety of ways in which divine being can be participated.

Human beings have trouble sharing this delight in true diversity. Some reject the diversity of creation on the grounds that all things must be valued in the same way (true diversity requires hierarchy, or else all things are the same again); others reject diversity because after sin its distortions result in oppression. Yet to come to know God as he is in his gratuitous gifting, we must be formed in receptivity to hierarchical diversity. Thus God gives this "beauty" of order not only to nature and to the blessed in heaven, but also the Church on earth.[13]

Second, God's gifting itself can be imitated by human beings. In creating and sustaining creatures, God acts both directly and in a mediated fashion; thus, for instance, God directly sustains the being of the tree, but he also works through nature's process of generation, involving the acorn, soil, sunlight, and so forth. Similarly, Christ himself bestows the sacramental grace of the Holy Spirit, and yet he does so through the mediation of human priests. As Aquinas says, in order

> that He might be portrayed in His works, not only according to what He is in Himself, but also according as He acts on others. . . . He established Order in her [the Church] so that some should deliver the sacraments to others, being thus made like God in their own way, as co-operating with God.[14]

---

13. Ibid., *respondeo*. On diversity in the Church, see Herwi Rikhof, "Thomas on the Church: Reflections on a Sermon," in *Aquinas on Doctrine*, eds. Thomas Weinandy, OFMCAP, Daniel Keating, and John Yocum (New York: T. & T. Clark, 2004), 211–2. Rikhof points out, "In his [Aquinas's] commentary on the Creed, he uses the term *diversa membra*. Within the one body this diversity does not disappear or become irrelevant. The diversity stays and has a purpose. Diversity would be meaningless if it were not ordered toward diverse acts. With regard to *singuli autem alter alteris membra* (Rom 12:5), Thomas remarks that Paul touches here upon the connection between the diversity and the common advantage (*utilitas*). He explains this phrase by saying that a member is called 'member of another' in so far as one member serves the other by its own proper activity. So, this diversity of members and acts is related to a common good on the one hand, and to the other members on the other" (211).

14. *Summa Theologiae, Suppl.* q. 34, a. 1, *respondeo*.

Is it only the priests and bishops, however, who are "being thus made like God" and "co-operating with God," since it is only the priests and bishops who possess hierarchical "order" in the Church? Certainly, in mediating God's action in believers, bishops/priests are "imitating" or participating in God's action in a unique way, as "the co-operators of God."[15] But the bishops'/priests' imitation of God's action serves the whole Church in its vocation of imitating and co-operating with God's action *ad extra*, the creation and perfecting of creatures. The recipients of the sacraments, who take on a new life and are nourished toward Christian perfection, imitate and co-operate with God through their fruitfulness in charity. Thus the hierarchical priesthood imitates and co-operates with the divine fruitfulness by enabling all believers to imitate and co-operate with the divine fruitfulness.

Since this imitation flows from sacramental grace, Aquinas defines the sacrament of Holy Orders as that "whereby man is ordained to the dispensation of the other sacraments,"[16] above all, to the Eucharist. He frequently observes that "the principal act of a priest is to consecrate the body and blood of Christ."[17] By the sacrament of Holy Orders, men are "appointed to lead others in Divine things"[18] and to exercise "a twofold action: the one, which is principal, over the true body of Christ; the other, which is secondary, over the mystical body of Christ."[19] The principal action that defines the priesthood is the Eucharistic celebration: as he says, "the second act depends on the first."[20] Thus, for Aquinas, the bishop's mission, while requiring more of the "secondary" action than is required of the priest, depends upon the bishop's "principal" action in the Eucharistic celebration. Aquinas describes bishops and priests as "instruments" of Christ's kenotic "outpouring" of grace: "the ministers of the Church are placed over others, not to confer anything on them by virtue of their own holiness (for this belongs to God alone), but as ministers, and as instruments, so to say, of the outpouring from the Head to the

---

15. See also *Suppl.*, q. 37, a. 1, which likewise cites Pseudo-Dionysius.

16. *Suppl.*, q. 35, a. 1.

17. *Suppl.*, q. 37, a. 5, as well as the *sed contra*.

18. *Suppl.*, q. 36, a. 1.

19. *Suppl.*, q. 36, a. 2, ad 1.

20. Ibid.

members."[21] This outpouring is eucharistic. As Aquinas says, following Pseudo-Dionysius, "the sacrament of Order is directed to the sacrament of the Eucharist, which is the sacrament of sacraments."[22]

Turning to the variety of orders, Aquinas argues similarly that the distinction between orders "is derived from their relation to the Eucharist."[23] For this reason he does not consider the bishop to possess a distinct "order" from the priest; both can celebrate the same Eucharist. The two are distinct because the bishop has a more perfect "power" within the same order, that is to say the power to ordain others, to consecrate religious, and to have a higher authority in the Church.[24] All distinctions between priests and deacons, as well as

---

21. *Suppl.*, q. 36, a. 3, ad 2.

22. *Suppl.*, q. 37, a. 2.

23. Ibid.

24. *Suppl.*, q. 40, a. 4. Aquinas goes on to explain, "Order may be understood in two ways. In one way as a sacrament, and thus, as already stated (q. 37, aa. 2, 4), every Order is directed to the sacrament of the Eucharist. Wherefore since the bishop has not a higher power than the priest, in this respect the episcopate is not an Order. In another way Order may be considered as an office in relation to certain sacred actions: and thus since in hierarchical actions a bishop has in relation to the mystical body a higher power than the priest, the episcopate is an Order" (*Suppl.*, q. 40, a. 5).

He adds in an answer to an objection, "Order considered as a sacrament which imprints a character is specially directed to the sacrament of the Eucharist, in which Christ Himself is contained, because by a character we are made like to Christ Himself. Hence although at his promotion a bishop receives a spiritual power in respect of certain sacraments, this power nevertheless has not the nature of a character. For this reason the episcopate is not an Order, in the sense in which an Order is a sacrament" (*Suppl.*, q. 40, a. 5, ad 2). This position of Aquinas receives some correction at the Second Vatican Council, which states, "The synod teaches that the fullness of the sacrament of order is conferred by episcopal consecration" and "The bishop, marked with the fullness of the sacrament of order, is 'the steward of the grace of the supreme priesthood,' especially in the Eucharist which he offers or which he ensures is offered, and by which the church continuously lives and grows" (*Lumen Gentium*, §§ 21 and 26, in *Decrees of the Ecumenical Councils*, vol. 2, *Trent to Vatican II*, ed. Norman P. Tanner, SJ, [Washington, DC: Georgetown University Press, 1990], 865, 870).

For discussion of Aquinas's position in light of the teaching of *Lumen Gentium*, see Guy Mansini, OSB, "Episcopal *Munera* and the Character of Episcopal Orders," *The Thomist* 66 (2002): 369–94, at 377 f.; Avery Dulles, SJ, *The Priestly Office*, 14, 44. On the distinction between "order" and "jurisdiction" see Mansini, "Episcopal *Munera* and the Character of Episcopal Orders," 76: "*Potestas ordinis* is given by sacrament, is for sacramental action, makes a man an instrument of Christ in such sacramental action, is stable and cannot be lost. Jurisdiction involves simple assignment (assignment of one's subjects) as by the instrument of the *missio canonica*, it is for ruling, it makes a man a vicar of Christ in teaching and ruling, and it is not stable in the same way *potestas ordinis* is and can be lost" (376). Regarding Vatican II's teaching, see Joseph Ratzinger, *Principles of Catholic Theology: Building Stones for a Fundamental Theology*, trans. Sister Mary Frances McCarthy, SND, (German 1982; San Francisco: Ignatius Press, 1987), 242–4 and 254–7, indebted to Henri de Lubac's historical thesis in *Corpus Mysticum*. Ratzinger comments

other "minor orders," have their source in the Eucharist because "the power of Order is directed either to the consecration of the Eucharist itself, or to some ministry in connection with this sacrament of the Eucharist."[25] Likewise, there is no need to differentiate orders according to sacraments other than the Eucharist. As Aquinas puts it a bit later, "The Orders are directed to the sacrament of the Eucharist chiefly, and to the other sacraments consequently, for even the other sacraments flow from that which is contained in that sacrament."[26] Lastly, Aquinas notes that each order, however minor, has as its "principal act" that action that is closest to the celebration of the Eucharist. This explains the hierarchy of the orders: "one Order ranks above another, in so far as one act is more nearly directed to that same sacrament."[27]

ORDERS IN THE *SUMMA CONTRA GENTILES*

Aquinas devotes chapters 74 to 77 in Book IV of the *Summa Contra Gentiles* to questions regarding the sacrament of Holy Orders. Of these four chapters, chapter 75 serves to explain the minor orders present in Aquinas's day—doorkeepers, readers, exorcists, acolytes, subdeacons, and deacons; chapter 76 focuses upon the reasons for the primacy of the Bishop of Rome; and chapter 77 treats the fact that sinful priests do not lose, by their sinful actions, the power to consecrate the sacraments. I will concentrate here on chapter 74, "On the Sacrament of Orders," which sets forth the principles of Aquinas's theology of orders.

In chapter 74, Aquinas proposes two ways of accounting for the existence of the ordained priesthood in the Church. Both flow from the nature of the sacraments. The first comes from the fact that sacramental actions mediate divine power through visible, corporeal signs. Since this is true, Aquinas reasons, those who perform sacramental actions should also be corporeal agents, rather than having the sacraments come directly from God or from angels. As he says,

---

that Vatican II's recognition of the bishop as possessing the "fullness of the sacrament of order" flows from grounding the theology of orders on the apostles (244).

25. *Suppl.*, q. 37, a. 2.

26. *Suppl.*, q. 37, a. 2, ad 3.

27. *Suppl.*, q. 37, a. 4.

"Therefore, the sacraments mentioned must be dispensed by visible men who have spiritual power."[28] Thus, sacramental unity with Christ requires not only the corporeal sign (the "thing," as it were), but also corporeal agents—men endowed with the spiritual power to communicate the power of Christ's Pasch. Aquinas sees the unity of the Church with Christ as a unity that flows inevitably through human bodiliness, even while in a certain sense transcending the limitations of that bodiliness through the sacramental sign.

Put another way: if God is going to make many human beings truly *one* in Christ, truly one with Christ so as to be the Body of Christ, then it might seem that such a miraculous action should be accomplished in a way that makes clear that human bodiliness no longer stands in the way of this new unity of the many in the Body of Christ. Angels or God himself might, on this view, best perform the sacraments, so that the new spiritual unity would be more fittingly and powerfully represented. Instead, however, God wills that this unity occur through the actions of, in Aquinas's words, "visible men who have spiritual power." These visible men, bishops and priests, make clear that the Church's spiritual unity as the Body of Christ flows through human bodiliness, which it does because Christ himself has a human body. The many become one with Christ, without thereby ceasing to be many; a spiritual union comes about that is not threatened by corporeality. Human beings are united to God through the incarnate Word in such a way that they both transcend their limitations by truly receiving a unity with Christ and do so in and through their human bodiliness, not solely through their souls.

The second way that Aquinas accounts for the existence of the ministerial priesthood revolves around Christ's gift of the power to participate in his saving Pasch. He gives this gift preeminently through the sacraments of faith, of which the principal ones are Baptism and the Eucharist. Aquinas cites in this regard Ephesians 5:25–26, "Christ loved the Church and gave himself up for her, that he might sanctify her, having cleansed her by the washing of water with the word"—a reference to the sanctifying power of Baptism— as well as the Gospel accounts of the Last Supper.[29] Do Christ's

---

28. *Summa Contra Gentiles*, Book IV, ch. 74 (p. 285).
29. Ibid., 286.

cleansing of the Church and his invitation to the Church to share in his sacrificial body and blood come to an end after Christ ascends to heaven? No. The New Testament makes clear that Christ charges his apostles with the sacramental mission of giving his gift. In this respect Aquinas quotes four biblical texts: 1 Corinthians 4:1, "This is how one should regard us, as servants of Christ and stewards of the mysteries of God"; Luke 22:19, "Do this in remembrance of me"; John 20:23, "If you forgive the sins of any, they are forgiven"; and Matthew 28:19, "Go therefore and make disciples of all nations, baptizing them."[30]

Yet, even if Christ's gift endures through the apostles, why should this mean that the bishop or priest, even as responsible for presiding over the celebration of the sacraments, possesses a distinctive spiritual power from that of the ordinary Christian? Why should not the spiritual power subsist solely in the sacramental action of the community as led by the bishop/priest, rather than requiring a distinctive spiritual power to subsist in the bishop/priest? Aquinas argues that the human agent cannot be so easily set to the side. The bishop/priest does not simply give an official stamp to sacramental celebrations by ensuring that they will not be marked by unorthodox faith or practice. Instead, to be (in Saint Paul's phrase) a "steward" of the "mysteries of God" is itself a distinctive participation in those "mysteries." At the Last Supper, Aquinas says, "since Christ was about to withdraw His bodily presence from the Church, it was necessary that Christ should establish other ministers in His place who would dispense the sacraments to the faithful."[31]

Do these other ministers require any particular power? Could the dispensing be extrinsic to what is dispensed? If the sacraments were mere things, such extrinsicism might be possible. Because the nature of the sacrament is inseparable from the particular action that effects the sacrament, however, Aquinas states that "the instrument must be proportionate to the agent. Hence, the ministers of Christ must be in conformity with Him."[32] Might such "conformity" simply involve the possession and manifestation of cruciform charity, so that a bishop/priest would be suited to give Christ's gift not by any

---

30. Ibid.
31. Ibid.
32. Ibid.

actual distinction from ordinary believers, but simply by manifestly
sharing in the faith and charity that all believers are called to possess?
In this case, the bishop's role would differ from the ordinary believer's
only in terms of administrative function; but Aquinas rejects this solution. The bishop/priest, in instrumentally giving Christ's gift, must
be likened to the true Giver (Christ) in a far more profound manner.

The Giver at the Last Supper, however, is God and man.
How can mere human beings dare to celebrate the Last Supper? Here
we arrive at the center of Aquinas's theology of the priesthood. He
points out that "Christ, as the Lord, by His very own authority and
power wrought our salvation, in that He was God and man: so far as
He was man, in order to suffer for our redemption; and, so far as He
was God, to make His suffering salutary for us."[33] In giving us the
gift of salvation, Christ, in the unity of his Person, acted through his
humanity and through his divinity. One can see how the ministers
can be configured to Christ's human nature: charity accomplishes this
configuration. But charitable human actions do not suffice for the
kind of actions that Christ's ministers, the priests and bishops, are
called to make. These actions, above all the celebration of the
Eucharist, are a participation in Christ's action not only with respect
to Christ as a charitable man, but also with respect to Christ as God.
The Last Supper is a human act and also a divine act, united in the
action of the incarnate Son of God. Thus, as Aquinas suggests, the
Eucharist teaches us that "the ministers of Christ must not only be
men, but must participate somehow in His divinity through some
spiritual power, for an instrument shares in the power of its principal
agent"[34]—especially a living "instrument" whose action the consecration of the Eucharist must also be. This "spiritual power," or sacramental "character,"[35] that distinguishes priests and bishops from

---

33. Ibid.

34. Ibid.

35. See Aquinas's discussion of sacramental "character," found in *Summa Theologiae*, III, q.
63. Following Augustine and Dionysius, Aquinas states that "the sacraments of the New Law
produce a character, in so far as by them we are deputed to the worship of God according to the
rite of the Christian religion. Wherefore Dionysius (*Eccl. Hier.* ii), after saying that God *by a kind
of sign grants a share of Himself to those that approach Him*, adds *by making them Godlike and
communicators of Divine gifts.* Now the worship of God consists either in receiving Divine gifts, or
in bestowing them on others. And for both these purposes some power is needed; for to bestow
something on others, active power is necessary; and in order to receive, we need a passive
power. . . . But it must be observed that this spiritual power is instrumental: as we have stated

ordinary believers is a certain participation in Christ's divine power, through the instrumental power of Christ's humanity, that enables them to give Christ's gift through their sacramental action. Their sacramental action participates uniquely in Christ's divine-human action through the spiritual power that they receive.

Aquinas identifies this "spiritual power" with the authority to which Saint Paul refers in warning the Corinthians to obey his teachings: "it is this power that the Apostle calls 'the power which the Lord hath given me unto edification and not unto destruction' (2 Corinthians 13:10)."[36] The sacraments of Baptism and the Eucharist are the foundation of a hierarchical priesthood possessed of a spiritual power that builds up the Church in ways that extend the Church's baptismal and eucharistic unity. Paul appeals to his apostolic authority or power, therefore, in teaching and governing, not solely in sanctifying, the Corinthians. Yet, Aquinas remarks upon the difference between Christ giving the gift of this spiritual power to apostles such as Paul, and the apostles giving the gift of this spiritual power to others. It makes sense that Christ can provide the apostles with a unique sharing in his power, but how can mere men share with other men a power that is more than human? Aquinas's inquiry assumes that Christ has given this spiritual power to the apostles so as to be passed on through the generations; otherwise the Church could not continue to be built up. In this regard he cites Matthew 28:20, "lo, I am with you always, to the close of the age" and Mark 13:37, "And what I say to you I say to all."

---

above (q. 62, a. 4) of the virtue which is in the sacraments. For to have a sacramental character belongs to God's ministers: and a minister is a kind of instrument, as the Philosopher says (*Polit.* i)" (III, q. 63, a. 2).

Aquinas goes on to observe that these active and passive sacramental characters "are nothing else than certain participations of Christ's Priesthood, flowing from Christ Himself" (III, q. 63, a. 3). Holy Orders imparts an active sacramental character, enabling the recipient to "bestow on others, things pertaining to Divine worship" (III, q. 63, a. 4). This theology of sacramental "character" enables Aquinas to distinguish between the common priesthood, pertaining to all the baptizing, and the hierarchical priesthood. Aquinas observes that "it is the sacrament of Order that pertains to the sacramental agents: for it is by this sacrament that men are deputed to confer sacraments on others: while the sacrament of Baptism pertains to the recipients, since it confers on man the power to receive the other sacraments of the Church; whence it is called the *door of the sacraments*" (III, q. 63, a. 6).

36. *Summa Contra Gentiles*, Book IV, ch. 74, p. 286.

Aquinas states, "This spiritual power from Christ, then, flows into the ministers of the Church."[37] But how could this occur? The answer is through the sacrament. Just as the sacrament of the Eucharist communicates what only Christ can give, so also does the sacrament of Holy Orders. The "spiritual power" that the apostles receive includes the power to share this spiritual power sacramentally, so that other men, too, might be able to give Christ's gift. In the other sacraments, Aquinas points out, spiritual changes are wrought in us by means of sensible signs. Regarding the spiritual power given the apostles, it follows that "this spiritual power also had to be passed on to men under certain sensible signs."[38] The apostles used bodily signs to pass on their spiritual power, and thereby they bestowed a sacrament, the sacrament of Holy Orders.

One recalls, however, that Christ directly chose his own Twelve disciples, and one of them betrayed him, while the others did little better. If the apostles pass on this unique spiritual power for building up the Church to other men, and these men pass it on to still other men (whose office receives the name *episkopos*), and so forth, can this method of transmission really conduce to building up the Church? Would not, on the contrary, things go from bad (the disciples) to worse (the bishops) once Christ no longer *directly* chooses the men who receive this unique spiritual power in the Church?[39] Relying on the divine goodness in bountifully bestowing the grace of the Holy Spirit, Aquinas notes that with respect to God's gifting, "if the power for some operation is conferred on one, there [will] be conferred also those things without which this operation cannot suitably be exercised."[40] In the case of the priesthood, what is needed for its suitable exercise is the grace of the Holy Spirit so as to configure the

---

37. Ibid., 287.

38. Ibid. For discussion of the importance of sensible signs, see Charles Morerod, OP, "John Paul II's Ecclesiology and St. Thomas Aquinas," in *John Paul II and St. Thomas Aquinas*, eds. Michael Dauphinais and Matthew Levering (Naples, FL: Sapientia Press, 2006), 47–51.

39. Aquinas thinks that the movement from the apostles down through the generations is to some degree a decline, since he holds that the apostles'—and to a lesser extent the Fathers'—temporal closeness to Christ gives them a spiritual preeminence. Cf. Serge-Thomas Bonino, OP, "The Role of the Apostles in the Communication of Revelation According to the *Lectura super Ioannem* of St. Thomas Aquinas," trans. Teresa Bede and Matthew Levering, in *Reading John with St. Thomas Aquinas*, eds. Michael Dauphinais and Matthew Levering (Washington, DC: The Catholic University of America Press, 2005), 318–46.

40. *Summa Contra Gentiles*, Book IV, ch. 74, 287.

priest to Christ's cruciform wisdom and self-giving service to others. As with the other sacraments, therefore, the sacrament of Holy Orders bestows a special grace that enables the recipient to attain the "end" of the sacrament.[41]

What is the "end" of the sacrament of Holy Orders, the service to which the priest is particularly called? Aquinas identifies the "end" as the giving of the sacraments. Priests are not called to just any service, but to a sacramental service. More precisely, the "end" is defined not simply by all the sacraments in general, but by the greatest sacrament, the Eucharist. To give the Eucharist is the ultimate reason for the priesthood. He explains that "among the sacraments, that which is most noble and tends most to complete the others is the sacrament of the Eucharist."[42] For Aquinas, then, the Eucharist is the only adequate lens for understanding the spiritual power of Holy Orders. As he puts it, characteristically citing Aristotle's *De anima*, "Therefore, the power of orders must be weighed chiefly by reference to this sacrament, for 'everything is denominated from its end.'"[43]

It is through the Eucharist that Aquinas explains the relationship of the spiritual power bestowed by the sacrament of Holy Orders to the sacraments that bestow the forgiveness of sins; namely, Baptism, Penance, and Extreme Unction. Why should priests have the power to forgive the sins of fellow believers, when priests are

---

41. Cf. Dermot Power, "The Priesthood and the Evangelical Counsels," *Communio* 23 (1996): 688–700, which focuses on Hans Urs von Balthasar's theology of the priesthood as a vocation of radical configuration to Christ by the grace of the Holy Spirit, which enables the priest to live out the evangelical counsels. See also for a theology of priestly celibacy, Henri de Lubac, sj, *The Motherhood of the Church*, trans. Sister Sergia Englund, ocd, (1971; San Francisco: Ignatius Press, 1982), 113–39; Avery Dulles, sj, *The Priestly Office*, 68–71.

42. *Summa Contra Gentiles*, Book IV, ch. 74, 287.

43. Ibid., 287–8. For further discussion and development of this point, see Henri de Lubac, sj, *The Splendor of the Church*, trans. Michael Mason (French 1953; San Francisco: Ignatius Press, 1986), 143–51. Citing a wide variety of sources including the *Summa Contra Gentiles*, de Lubac remarks, "To hold in their own hands the Eucharist—that is the supreme prerogative of those who form the hierarchy in the Church and are 'the ministers of Christ and the dispensers of the mysteries of God.' The hierarchy's 'most priestly action,' and the supreme exercise of its power, lies in consecrating Christ's body and thus perpetuating the work of the Redemption—in offering the 'sacrifice of praise,' which is the only one pleasing to God. In a broad sense, the whole Christian people is associated with that power at that point, and that is the meaning of St. Leo's words that the anointing of the Sovereign Pontiff 'reaches to the very extremities of the whole body of the Church.' That exercise of the hierarchical power, in the name of Christ, is one which constitutes the hierarchy's 'primary and most august function.' So, if we are to understand the role of the hierarchy—which is to understand the Church—we must consider the hierarchy via the action by which this function is carried out" (147–9).

sinners too? In this regard, Aquinas first employs an analogy from the realm of physical power. "Fire," he points out, "has the power both to pass its form on to another, and to dispose that other for the reception of the form."[44] In order to catch fire, something must become hot. As Aquinas states in philosophical terms, one would expect that "the same power which grants a perfection" is also that "which prepares matter for the reception of that perfection."[45] The perfection granted by the spiritual power of Holy Orders is ultimately that of confecting and bestowing the Eucharist. Thus, one should expect the spiritual power of Holy Orders, like a spiritual "fire," to extend also to preparing believers for properly receiving the Eucharist.

Proper reception of the Eucharist requires above all rightly ordered love. Aquinas observes that "a believer is made ready for the reception of this sacrament [the Eucharist] and in harmony with it by his freedom from sin; otherwise, he cannot be united spiritually with that Christ to whom he is sacramentally conjoined by the reception of this sacrament."[46] The ecclesial unity in Christ established by the Eucharist, and correspondingly by the sacrament of Holy Orders, requires holiness; lacking holiness there is no full incorporation into Christ. It follows that "the power of orders must extend itself to the remission of sins by the dispensation of those sacraments which are ordered to the remission of sins";[47] namely, Baptism and Penance. Aquinas suggests that this connection both illumines, and is illumined by, scripture:

> This, indeed, is the power we understand by the "keys" about which our Lord said to Peter: "I will give to thee the keys of the kingdom of heaven" (Mt 16:19). For to every man heaven is closed or opened by this: he is subject to sin, or he is cleansed from sin; hence, too, the use of these keys is called "to bind and to loose," namely, from sins.[48]

What might seem like an overbearing assumption of power by the priesthood—the power of excommunication and the forgiveness of sins—thus appears in its true eucharistic light.

---

44. *Summa Contra Gentiles*, Book IV, ch. 74, 288.
45. Ibid.
46. Ibid.
47. Ibid.
48. Ibid.

Conclusion

Quoting Aquinas's *Commentary on the Epistle to the Hebrews*, the *Catechism of the Catholic Church* observes,

> The redemptive sacrifice of Christ is unique, accomplished once for all; yet it is made present in the Eucharistic sacrifice of the Church. The same is true of the one priesthood of Christ; it is made present through the ministerial priesthood without diminishing the uniqueness of Christ's priesthood: "Only Christ is the true priest, the others being only his ministers." (CCC 1545)

The role of these priestly ministers is to enable the whole Church to share eucharistically in Christ's self-offering in the Spirit to the Father. Christ alone is our "great high priest" (Hebrews 4:14), "holy, blameless, unstained, separated from sinners, exalted above the heavens" (Hebrews 7:26). Christ bore our sins "once for all when he offered up himself" (Hebrews 7:27), so that "by a single offering he has perfected for all time those who are sanctified" (Hebrews 10:14).

Christ's priests, then, do not receive a power that is strictly their own. Rather, as we have seen, they receive a participation in Christ's power, so that others might in turn be united to Christ's eucharistic self-offering, a unity that involves and requires sanctifying, teaching, and governing. Far from imagining that all members of the hierarchical priesthood are holy, however, Aquinas observes that "our Lord has good and wicked ministers or servants."[49] How then can we trust that God will preserve the Church's mediation of Christ's self-offering? For Aquinas the answer possesses the simplicity of faith. Namely, the Church's mediation of the cruciform pattern of Christ's self-offering is Christ's work in the Spirit, not ours. As Saint Paul puts it, "God is faithful, by whom you were called into the fellowship of his Son, Jesus Christ our Lord" (1 Corinthians 1:9).

---

49. *Summa Theologiae* III, q. 82, a. 5. In II-II, q. 100, aa. 1–2, Aquinas decries the sin of simony—the practice of receiving "money for the spiritual grace of the sacraments"—and his manner of enumerating this sin indicates his awareness of its prevalence.

Chapter 8

Aquinas on the Sacrament of Marriage

Joseph W. Koterski, sj

The *Summa Theologiae* was left unfinished at Saint Thomas's death. Thus, we do not have from this source an account of his theology of Marriage in the way that we do have his reflections on the sacraments of Baptism, Confirmation, the Eucharist, and (at least in part) Penance. But materials from his commentary on the *Sentences* (written some twenty years earlier) and from the relevant chapters in Books III and IV of the *Summa Contra Gentiles* were taken up by Thomas's disciples—presumably Reginald of Piperno—for the production of the *Supplement* to the *Summa Theologiae*, questions 41–68. As a result, there are certain difficulties about using this part of the *Summa Theologiae* to discuss the mature views of Aquinas on Marriage or to assess the developments within Aquinas's own thinking about the sacraments in the period between the composition of the *Sentences* commentary and that of the two *summae*. But even though one must speak about the Thomistic understanding of Marriage with some qualifications because of the state of the texts, it is also clear that those who compiled the *Supplement* tried diligently to be faithful to Thomas's earlier writings on the subject, even if they were not able (or did not feel free) to advance it in the ways that he might have done himself, given the developments in his thinking about some of the other sacraments and the contributions that he made thereby for the advance of the theology of the sacraments in general.

In this chapter I will take up all the texts that are available to us and will address here just one aspect of the available Thomistic material on Marriage; namely, the duality of his approach to the topic through natural law and sacramentality. While a certain portion of the material on Marriage in the *Summa Theologiae* has the flavor of canon law,[1] there is also throughout that body of material a recurrent attention to questions about the status of Marriage in regard to natural law and sacramentality. The topic of the questions that form the opening gambit of this treatise reflect this duality: "Of the Sacrament of Matrimony as directed to a duty [*officium*] of nature" (q. 41) and "Of Matrimony as a Sacrament" (q. 42). Thereafter, the topics for the questions that constitute this treatise are for the most part canonical, disciplinary, and pastoral in nature: betrothal (q. 43), the definition of Marriage (q. 44), Marriage consent (q. 45), the role of oath and of intercourse in addition to consent (q. 46), compulsory and conditional assent (q. 47), the object of the consent (q. 48), the goods of Marriage (q. 49), impediments in general (q. 50), and then various specific impediments: error (q. 51), the condition of slavery (q. 52), vows and orders (q. 53), consanguinity (q. 54), affinity (q. 55), spiritual relationship (q. 56), legal adoption (q. 57), impotence, frenzy or madness, incest, defective age (q. 58), disparity of worship (q. 59), wife-murder (q. 60), solemn vows (q. 61), fornication after consummation (q. 62); then other canonical questions: second Marriages (q. 63), payment of the Marriage debt (q. 64), plurality of wives (q. 65), bigamy (q. 66), the bill of divorce (q. 67), and illegitimate children (q. 68). While a good number of these topics also raise questions of a philosophical and theological nature, with an occasional return to the topics of natural law and sacramentality, I want to confine myself here to the explicit discussion of the sacramentality of Marriage and the correlative discussion of Marriage from the viewpoint of natural law as a pair of topics useful for grasping Thomas's distinctive thinking on this subject.

First, we should be mindful of two points about the historical context of Aquinas's work: 1) the important developments in sacramental theology being made during the period of medieval scholasticism, and especially his own contributions to the position that the sacraments are not just signs of sacred things but signs that bring

---

1. See the extensive treatment of this question in Seamus P. Heaney, *The Development of the Sacramentality of Marriage from Anselm of Laon to Thomas Aquinas* (S.T.D. diss.; Washington, DC: The Catholic University of America Press, 1963).

about the grace that they signify, and 2) the recovery of Aristotle's natural philosophy in the twelfth and thirteenth centuries, and especially Thomas's ground-breaking work in the area of natural law. What is especially relevant here is Thomas's development of a way in which to use the notion of "nature" normatively in ethics. He regards the orientation of each natural kind toward its specific set of ends that is found in all things, including human beings, to be a result of the divine creation of all things according to various natural kinds. So considered, "nature" is a principle for explaining why things are what they are and why they operate as they do, but also as a reliable way by which we can know these things. Thomas's confidence in the ability of human reason to discern the end that God has implanted in human nature permits him to say that human beings can and should participate in providential reasoning about how to attain the ends for which they are made by ascertaining from reflection on our nature what sorts of actions are in accord and likely to assist in the attainment of this end, and which contradict or are likely to frustrate that end. As Russell Hittinger and Fulvio Di Blasi have reminded us in their recent works on natural law,[2] the Thomistic theory of natural law should not be seen as primarily a work of philosophy independent of theology, but as philosophically informed use of reason in moral theology. That his theory of natural law should play some role in his thoughts on Marriage is thus not surprising and to be expected.

Throughout Thomas's treatise on the sacraments we see him alert both to the theme of the sacraments as *signs* of *sacred things* that bring us *grace* and to the questions being raised in his day about how the sacraments are efficacious, about just what counts as a sacrament of the New Law, and about how these sacraments are related to the sacraments of the Old Law as well as to human nature in general. Many of his positions on these questions will provide the bulwark of what the Council of Trent later codified.

Central to Aquinas's view of the sacraments is his stress on the fact that the sacraments are signs, instituted by Christ, to give

---

2. Russell Hittinger, *The First Grace: Recovering the Natural Law in a Post-Christian World* (Wilmington, DE: ISI, 2003); and Fulvio Di Blasi, *God and the Natural Law* (South Bend, IN: St. Augustine's Press, 2006).

grace, by bringing about what they signify.[3] The part of the treatise on the sacraments that Thomas composed for the *Summa* constitutes the second half of the *tertia pars*. The first section (qq. 1–59) is devoted to "the mysteries of the Incarnate Word," from which, in Aquinas's view, the sacraments of the Church "have their efficacy."[4] Throughout this treatise we find him treating the sacraments as genuinely capable of sanctifying us, that is, as real means of grace. Earlier in the *Summa*, as part of the general account of moral theory that includes his natural law theory, he had covered the freely chosen acts that human beings need to make and the virtues that can assist us, both those that come about only by a divine gift and those that we can also develop on the basis of our natural abilities. Like the general treatments of grace and of law, the section on the sacraments shows us Aquinas's convictions 1) that the sacraments of the New Law are a crucial part of the assistance that God has designed to help us in the quest for beatitude and 2) that they build on the sacraments of the Old Law as well as on certain aspects of human nature known by reflection on the needs of human nature.

It is extremely significant that Aquinas's treatise on the sacraments comes after his treatment of Christ and the nature of his saving actions. The efficacy of the sacraments, in his view, comes directly from Christ through the Church. Sacraments are "sacred signs," a notion that Aquinas borrows from Augustine; that is, signs of a sacred reality that is at work to sanctify man.[5] By a kind of shorthand, one might speak simply about the sacraments as signs that bring about what they signify, but it is always important to bear in mind even when using this shorthand to remember what the abbreviated form of speaking is supposed to convey in its fullness. The Christological context in which Aquinas places his account of the sacraments makes it clear that he believes that it is Christ himself who acts through the sacraments of the Church that he founded, or to use his own phrasing, through each "sacrament of the New Law." In the prologue to the *tertia pars*, Aquinas had commented: "Our Savior, the Lord Jesus . . . showed himself to us as the way of the truth by which

---

3. See the extensive comments on this theme in Brian Davies, *The Thought of Thomas Aquinas* (Oxford: Clarendon Press, 1992), esp. 346–61.

4. III, q. 60, prol.

5. See III, q. 60, a. 2.

it is now possible for us to arrive at the resurrection and the happiness of immortal life." For Thomas, the study of Christ the Savior is indispensable for completing the task in theology that he has set for himself; regarding the material under study here, the divine assistance that Christ provides is indispensable for us to reach the final end of human life. The Christological dimension of Aquinas's general theory of the sacraments is thus an important part of his reflections on Marriage as a sacrament, as for instance when he writes: "Although Matrimony is not conformed to Christ's Passion as regards pain, it is as regards charity, whereby he suffered for the Church, who was to be united to him as his spouse."[6] One also sees this clearly in the corresponding sections of the *Summa Contra Gentiles* and the *Supplement.*[7]

For Thomas, some of the sacraments of the New Law were prefigured by sacraments of the Old Law—Baptism, for instance, by circumcision; the Eucharist by the meal of the Paschal lamb; Ordination by the consecration of the high priest; and Penance by the various forms of purification described in the Old Testament. Interestingly, Thomas sees the sacraments of the Old Covenant as the external expressions of faith (*protestationes fidei*) in the *future* Savior, whose Passion would be the source of the efficacy of these Old Testament sacraments.[8] Marriage, too, has various prefigurations as a sign that is used throughout the Old Testament for God's relationship with the people of Israel. But with this case, perhaps more than with any other, Aquinas presses the question about whether Marriage is a sacrament in conjunction with his efforts to understand Marriage in terms of the needs of human nature and an explicit discussion of natural law.

Jean-Pierre Torrell, OP, rightly stresses that Aquinas's doctrine of the sacraments is characterized by a sustained analogy between bodily life and sacramental life.[9] This analogy works as well as it does for Aquinas precisely by his attentiveness to human nature in its

---

6. *Suppl.*, q. 42, a.1, ad 3.

7. See *Summa Contra Gentiles* (SCG), IV, q. 78; and ST III, *Suppl.*, q. 42, esp. a. 3.

8. See Eric Luijten's *Sacramental Forgiveness as a Gift of God: Thomas Aquinas on the Sacrament of Penance* (Leuven: Peeters, 2003), esp. 176—and the discussion there of passages such as ST I-II, q. 102, a. 5, ad 3.

9. Jean-Pierre Torrell, OP, *Aquinas's Summa: Background, Structure, and Reception*, trans. Benedict M. Guevin, OSB (Washington, DC: The Catholic University of America Press, 2005), 61.

social as well as its individual dimensions, as his treatise on the natural moral law recurrently makes clear. Using that analogy, Thomas notes (at *Summa Theologiae* [ST] III, q. 65, a. 1) that human life is marked both by the kind of growth that perfects an individual person and also by the type that pertains to the community, "for man is by nature a social animal." For Thomistic sacramental theology, one can well raise the question of how this works for each of the sacraments, but it is clear that it proves quite helpful for understanding Aquinas's account of Marriage. Independently of the question about Marriage as a sacrament, it is a natural institution, designed by God as part of the providential plan of the eternal law and accessible to us as part of the natural law, so as to help us to achieve the social end that is the propagation of the species as well as to contribute to the maturation of individuals. Aquinas holds that the human person, as individual and as social, is perfected through Marriage both bodily and spiritually. We can see this point as he argues for it in the *Summa Contra Gentiles*:

> In the human species, offspring require not only nourishment for the body, as in the case of other animals, but also education for the soul. For other animals naturally possess their own kinds of prudence, whereby they are enabled to take care of themselves. But a man lives by reason, which he must develop by lengthy, temporal experience so that he may achieve prudence. Hence, children must be instructed by parents who are already experienced people. Nor are they able to receive such instruction as soon as they are born, but after a long time, and especially after they have reached the age of discretion. Moreover, a long time is needed for this instruction. Then, too, because of the impulsion of the passions, through which prudent judgment is vitiated, they require not merely instruction but correction.[10]

In this text he reviews some of the ways in which Marriage and the social bond that it creates can be perfective for an individual. To this consideration Aquinas adds an equally commonsensical consideration when he urges that a woman is not able to do this task alone but needs a husband:

> In the human species, it is not enough, as in the case of birds, to devote a small amount of time to bringing up offspring, for a long period of life is

---

10. SCG III, ch. 122.

required. Hence, since among all animals it is necessary for male and female to remain together as long as the work of the father is needed by the offspring, it is natural to the human being for the man to establish a lasting association with a certain woman, over no short period of time. Now, we call this society matrimony. Therefore, matrimony is natural for man, and promiscuous performance of the sexual act outside matrimony is contrary to man's good. For this reason it must be a sin.

The first question on Marriage in the *Supplement* to the *Summa Theologiae* (q. 41) takes up precisely the same points. Matrimony is not "natural," he argues, in the way in which the movements of sub-rational beings are "necessary because of their natures," but rather in the sense of "natural" that is pertinent to the will and the choices that it makes in its freedom, such as the way in which acts of virtue and the virtues themselves are rightly called "natural."[11] The principal end to which our nature inclines us is the good of the offspring, "for nature intends not only the begetting of offspring, but also its education and development until it reach the perfect state of man as man and that is the state of virtue." In his view, a child is not likely to be brought up and educated well unless suitable particular individuals play this role, but this is not likely to be the case unless a particular man and a particular woman are sufficiently tied together in the way that matrimony (the specifics of cultural differences notwithstanding)[12] unites them, both for the good of the offspring and for "the mutual services that married persons render one another in household matters." There is, of course, nothing surprising here. The argument is dry and reserved—one might even say minimal— but accurate. The rearing of rational creatures requires more care than the rearing of other creatures.[13] Not only do the rational creatures being reared have needs, but so do those who are doing the rearing. While this argument is articulated in terms of natural law rather than,

---

11. ST *Suppl.*, q. 41, c. For this and the following quotations, I cite the translation by the Fathers of the English Dominican Province, *Summa Theologiae*, vol. 3 (New York: Benziger, 1948), 2711 ff.

12. ST *Suppl.*, q. 41, a.1, ad 3: "According to the Philosopher (*Ethic.*, vii), *human nature is not unchangeable as the Divine nature is.* Hence things that are of natural law vary according to the various states and conditions of man: although those which naturally pertain to things Divine nowise vary."

13. This comparison between human child-rearing and the rearing involved in other species of animals is developed at great length in *Suppl.*, q. 41, a. 1, ad 1.

say, in personalist terms (for instance, in terms of the mutual love of spouses and even in terms of the self-gift that is at the essence of the marital commitment), there remains something of good sense here that can become a sound basis for the development of a personalist view of this matter.

Some obligations that arise from the natural moral law bind everyone because they command what is required for the perfection of every individual. But, for Thomas, the inclination under consideration here is not necessarily a duty (*officium*) for every individual. Marriage needs to exist for "the perfection of the community," but it does not bind every member of the community. The example that he provides in question 41, article 2, is by way of reference to the contemplative life, which he also thinks to be something necessary for the human community but something difficult for married people. While I could comment on the difficulties of trying to contemplate even for a religious, I leave the discussion of the more advanced point about the difficulties of contemplation by the married for those with greater experience.[14]

In the next two articles, he takes up the question of whether marital intercourse is always sinful and whether it is ever meritorious. On the question of whether intercourse is always sinful, his answer is clearly negative, and he makes a careful distinction with regard to merit. Although Thomas does not treat the matter in quite the way that we might find in, say, John Paul II's theology of the body, there is a great clarity to his response, and even some of the fierceness that we might expect of a Dominican in combating any hint of Manicheism, whether in the Albigensian forms known to the Middle Ages or to the Gnostic forms more typical of our own age:

> If we suppose the corporeal nature to be created by the good God, we cannot hold that those things which pertain to the preservation of the corporeal nature and to which nature inclines, are altogether evil: wherefore, since the inclination to beget an offspring whereby the specific nature is

---

14. The response to objection 2 is revealing: "A lawful occupation about lower things distracts the mind, so that it is not fit for actual union with God; and this is especially the case in carnal intercourse, wherein the mind is withheld by the intensity of pleasure. For this reason those who have to contemplate Divine things or handle sacred things are enjoined [in the texts cited in the objection itself] not to have to do with their wives for that particular time; and it is in this sense that the Holy Ghost, as regards the actual revelation of hidden things, did not touch the hearts of the prophets at the time of the marriage act" (*Suppl.*, q. 41, a. 3, ad 2).

preserved is from nature, it is impossible to maintain that the act of begetting children is altogether unlawful so that it be impossible to find the
mean of virtue therein: unless we suppose, as some are mad enough to
assert, that corruptible things were created by an evil god, whence perhaps
the opinion mentioned in the text is derived (*In IV Sent.*, d. 26): wherefore
this is a most wicked heresy.[15]

Likewise, in a response to one of the objections, Aquinas clearly
distinguishes between the phenomenon of shame and that of guilt
in a way that in one way is not unlike that of John Paul II's treatment
of the subject in *Love and Responsibility*: "The shamefulness of
concupiscence that always accompanies the marriage act is a shamefulness not of guilt but of the punishment inflicted for the first sin,
inasmuch as the lower powers and the members do not obey reason."[16]

His answer to the query about merit brings the natural law
considerations that have been prominent in this question into correla-
tion with the topic of virtue, in much the same way that we see his
general treatise on natural law connection to the subject of virtue:

Since no act proceeding from a deliberate will is indifferent, . . . the marriage act is always either sinful or meritorious in one who is in a state of
grace. For if the motive for the marriage act be a virtue, whether of justice
that they may render the debt, or of religion, that they may beget children
for the worship of God, it is meritorious. But if the motive be lust, yet
not excluding the marriage blessings, namely, that he would by no means
be willing to go to another woman, it is a venial sin; while if he exclude
the marriage blessings, so as to be disposed to act in like manner with any
woman, it is a mortal sin. And nature cannot move without being either
directed by reason, and thus it will be an act of virtue, or not so directed,
and then it will be an act of lust.[17]

As before, there are no surprises here. In some quarters, the phrase
"rendering the marriage debt" may be subjected to ridicule as overly

---

15. *Suppl.*, q. 41, a. 3, c.

16. *Suppl.*, q. 41, a. 3, ad 3. In the reply to the sixth objection, we also get a relevant
comment: "The excess of passions that corrupts virtue not only hinders the act of reason, but also
destroys the order of reason. The intensity of pleasure in the marriage act does not do this, since,
although for the moment man is not being directed, he was previously directed by his reason."
See Karol Wojtyła, *Love and Responsibility*, trans. H. T. Willets (New York: Farrar, Strauss and
Giroux, 1981), 174–93.

17. *Suppl.*, q. 41, a. 4, c.

minimalist or as if implying the reluctant performance of some distasteful act. But I think that such interpretations unfairly import considerations that might be true in a particular case but that are not true universally. A more charitable interpretation of this phrase would have us interpret his claim here in terms of the need to honor the commitment that spouses have made to one another as fully as possible and without qualification.

Immediately following this treatment of Marriage from the viewpoint of natural law and virtue we find the question, much debated in pre-tridentine theology, about whether Marriage is a sacrament. Aquinas gives an affirmative reply, to be sure, but he brings to bear several considerations that might be surprising, including reference in question 42, article 2, to the natural law and to the distinction between sacraments of the Old Law and those of the New Law. One sees here that the editors of the *Supplement* have been faithful to Thomas's inclination to yoke together the questions of sacramentality and natural law. Aquinas pursues the question of whether Marriage is a sacrament[18] by speculating about whether Marriage ought to have been instituted even before the first sin. The assumption in play in raising the question in this way was apparently that Marriage may only have been instituted subsequent to the Fall as a way in which to manage the concupiscence that was the result of original sin.[19] The argument for this view would presumably be that there was no need for Marriage prior to sin, since prior to sin there would have been no concupiscence. Thomas responds by a careful three-fold distinction: 1) Independently of original sin, Marriage is naturally oriented to procreation, and there is need for procreation regardless of sin, so God instituted Marriage prior to the original sin. 2) But after the Fall, the natural law required the institution of Marriage, and the law of Moses further specified it, as a way to heal the inherited wound of sin.[20] 3) In the New Covenant Christ instituted Marriage as a way to represent the mystery of the union of

---

18. *Sent.*, bk 4, d. 26, q. 2.

19. That Thomas does agree with this assumption in part is clear, as in this remark: "A sacrament denotes a sanctifying remedy against sin offered to man under sensible signs. Wherefore, since this is the case in matrimony, it is reckoned among the sacraments." (ST *Suppl.*, q. 42, a. 1, c.).

20. See esp. *Suppl.*, q. 42, a. 2, c. and ad 1.

Christ and the Church and to bring to spouses the graces of participation in this union. It is by the fact that it serves the function of being an image of this sort that it is a sacrament of the New Law. He also comments briefly on other beneficial effects that Marriage has, such as friendship of the spouses and mutual help. The earlier institution of Marriage as a *remedium* carries forward into its sacramentality—the *remedium* for concupiscence becomes included by the way in which it represents the Christ-Church union.

The telling point, of course, about whether matrimony is a sacrament of the Church is whether matrimony does what the sacraments in general are to do, that is, whether and how the sacraments are the means by which Christ brings about the grace that they signify. In the course of his discussion of this point, Thomas makes clear that Marriage (like the other sacraments) is more than just a sign of sacred things, and he makes clear that one of the sacred things of which it is a sign is something that it does not bring about: "The union of Christ with the Church is not the reality contained in this sacrament—and no sacrament causes a reality of that kind."[21]

The clearest statements on the question of what Marriage does bring about seem to me to be in the *Summa Contra Gentiles*, where he writes about the question of efficacy precisely in terms of including those who marry within the union of Christ and the Church. In the course of his argument he finds indissolubility to be a mark of sacramental Marriage:

> And because the sacraments effect that of which they are made signs, one must believe that in this sacrament a grace is conferred on those marrying, and that by this grace they are included in the union of Christ and the Church, which is most especially necessary to them, that in this way in fleshly and earthly things they may purpose not to be disunited from Christ and the Church.
>
> Since then the union of husband and wife gives a sign of the union of Christ and the Church, that which makes the sign must correspond to that whose sign it is. Now the union of Christ and the Church is a union of one to one to be held forever. For there is one Church, as the Canticle (6:8) says: 'One is my dove, my perfect one.' And Christ will never be separated from his Church, for he himself says: 'Behold I am with you all days, even to the consummation of the world' (Mt. 28:20); and further, 'we shall

---

21. *Suppl.*, q. 42, a. 1, ad 4.

be always with the Lord (1 Thess. 4:16), as the Apostle says. Necessarily then, matrimony as a sacrament of the Church is a union of one man to one woman to be held indivisibly, and this is included in the faithfulness by which the man and wife are bound to one another.[22]

In the corresponding sections of the *Sentences* and the *Supplement*, the reason for regarding Marriage as being a sacrament of the New Law also tends to be stated in terms of the graces that it confers. After noting some of the disputes on this point, Aquinas concludes that matrimony, inasmuch as it is contracted in the faith of Christ, is able to confer the grace that enables us to do what Marriage requires, for wherever God gives us a faculty to do something, God also gives the helps by which one can do it well.[23]

Whatever we make of the textual problems that come from having to make use of materials that were gathered from Thomas's other writings after his death, Thomas and his editors have generated a highly consistent framework for the discussion of many more detailed questions about Marriage by recurrently setting forth natural law and sacramentality as the proper context within which to consider Marriage. After all, for Thomas, grace builds on nature, and it is no surprise that we should find this to be the case in regard to Marriage.

---

22. SCG IV, a. 78, 4–5.
23. See ST *Suppl.*, q. 42, a. 3, c.

Chapter 9

The Role of *Solemnitas* in the Liturgy According to Saint Thomas Aquinas

Sister Thomas Augustine Becker, OP

Who is like to you among the gods, O Lord? Who is like to you magnificent in holiness? O terrible in renown, worker of wonders, when you stretched out your right hand, the earth swallowed them! In your mercy you led the people you redeemed; in your strength you guided them to your holy dwelling.

Exodus 15:11–3

The Eucharistic Blood revives the flower of the royal image in us. By it, the soul is purified, ignited by it, our intellect becomes brighter than fire, our soul more magnificent than gold. This Blood has been shed for us and has opened heaven for us. . . . Let us imagine that someone plunges his hand or tongue into the molten gold; it would suddenly be gilded.

    As great, perhaps even greater still, are the effects which these present gifts have on the soul.

Saint John Chrysostom

The principal means of obtaining the grace necessary for eternal life in beatitude are the sacraments of the Church instituted by Christ himself. We know the sacraments cause the grace they signify *ex opere operato* by the power of God. Nonetheless, it is not simply right to say that a sacrament bestows its effects automatically, for there is also need for the recipient of the sacrament, with devotion and faith, to accept willingly God's offering of his very life.[1] In this respect the disposition of the heart and mind of the recipient of a sacrament is the hinge, if you will, upon which the work of God in his sacraments

---

A special thanks to Joseph Koterski, SJ, for his encouragement and guidance, which have proved invaluable to me in writing this essay.

1. Josef Pieper, *In Search of the Sacred,* trans. Lothar Krauth (San Francisco: Ignatius Press, 1991), 38.

depends.[2] Without the proper dispositions, a person walks away from the reception of a sacrament at best the same person, at worst, a lesser one. As a result, this work of God—the transformation of the human soul by the power of grace that is the very reason for which the sacraments were instituted—is, to some degree, thwarted.

The desired objective of the sacraments is not only the transformation of the human soul (albeit incrementally in the life of most believers), but is also, and according to Saint Thomas chiefly, Christ's worship of the Father in us.[3] Pleasing worship of God depends upon the proper dispositions of heart and mind of the one offering worship.[4] The role played by the interior disposition of the participant in achieving these "two inseparable objectives of the liturgy, sanctification [of man] and homage [paid to God],"[5] is the general focus of this chapter. I will also consider what Saint Thomas has to say about the psychological dimension of the liturgy and its effect on the quality of the participation of the faithful. Specifically, I will look at Thomas's use of *solemnitas* and his understanding of its relationship to offering acceptable worship and the fruitful reception of grace in the use of the sacraments. The importance of *solemnitas* applies to all the liturgies of the Church's sacraments, but for the most part I will examine the question in light of the liturgy of the Eucharist. As Saint Thomas says, "the whole mystery of our salvation is comprised in this sacrament, [and] therefore is it performed with greater solemnity than the other sacraments."[6]

Throughout the chapter, the dispositions proper to acceptable worship and the fruitful reception of grace will be treated together, because they are essentially the same and because such treatment is fitting insofar as the celebration of the sacraments is ordained to both

---

2. *Mediator Dei*, no. 31.

3. David Berger, *Thomas Aquinas and the Liturgy*, trans. Christopher Grosz (Naples, FL: Sapientia Press, 2004), 87.

4. This is not meant to imply that the worship offered by Christ's perfect sacrifice once and for all is in any way diminished by the manner in which man approaches the sacraments.

5. Berger, *Thomas Aquinas and the Liturgy*, 87.

6. *Summa Theologiae* III, q. 83, a. 4: "quia in hoc sacramento totum mysterium nostrae salutis comprehenditur, ideo prae ceteris sacramentis cum maiori solemnitate agitur." For quotations from the *Summa Theologiae*, I have used the translation by the Fathers of the English Dominican Province published in 1920 (Westminster, MD: Christian Classics, 1981) together with the Web site: http://krystal.op.cz/sth/sth.php.

the worship of God and the sanctification of man.[7] While inquiry
into the mysterious ways in which the heart and mind are moved is
bound to be imprecise in some ways, the fundamental and universal
characteristics of human nature do allow for some conclusions to
be drawn that are not easily dismissed on the grounds of subjectivity,
cultural differences, and the like. It is in this regard that I will consider the important role of solemnity in the liturgy.

INTERIOR DISPOSITION—*DEVOTIO*

The keeping of the New Law depends on the indwelling of the Holy
Spirit, and thus the interior landscape of man becomes the focus for
religious observance.[8] Since the coming of Christ and the institution
of the sacraments of the New Law, true worship together with the
sanctification of man take place primarily within the interior of man
in his heart and mind,[9] and yet according to Thomas, religion
comprises both interior and exterior acts.[10] The interior acts of religion are devotion and prayer; the chief sacrifice offered by man to
God is an inward sacrifice in the form of devotion and prayer.[11]
Devotion and prayer engage both the will and the intellect, but it is
devotion, the "will to give oneself readily to things concerning the
service of God,"[12] that is the principal act of religion.[13] It is fostered
by considering such things as the goodness of God and man's own
shortcomings and weaknesses, and it involves submission and

---

7. See Liam G. Walsh, OP, "Liturgy in the Theology of St. Thomas," *The Thomist* 38 (1974).

8. I-II q. 108, a. 1: "I answer that . . . the New Law consists chiefly in the grace of the
Holy Ghost, which is shown forth by faith that worketh through love." ad. 1: "The kingdom of
God consists chiefly in internal acts."

9. This is not to suggest that the sacrifice of Christ on the cross and its re-presentation at
Mass are eclipsed by man's offering, but only that it is not the focus of this discussion.

10. II-II, q. 82, Preamble. The external acts of religion include adoration, sacrifice, oblations,
and tithes.

11. II-II, q. 85 a. 3, ad 2.

12. II-II, q. 82 a. 1, co.

13. II-II, q. 83 a. 3, ad 1: "therefore religion, which is in the will, directs the acts of the other
powers to the reverence of God. Now among the other powers of the soul the intellect is the
highest, and the nearest to the will; and consequently after devotion which belongs to the will,
prayer which belongs to the intellective part is the chief of the acts of religion, since by it religion
directs man's intellect to God." See also, ST II-II q. 104, a. 3 ad. 1: "and in so far as it proceeds
from reverence for God, it comes under religion, and pertains to devotion, which is the principal
act of religion."

surrender to God.[14] Devotion is not only the first and principal act of
religion; it is also the "necessary condition to all its secondary acts."[15]
Additionally, it is the "first, basic psychological attitude which is the
fruit of the virtue of religion."[16] In short, devotion is the disposition
of heart essential to the exercise of the virtue of religion, which
includes efficacious participation in the sacraments.[17]

Not surprisingly, then, a survey of the *Summa* reflects the
importance placed by Thomas on the role of devotion in the religious
life of man. Before considering our main focus, the relationship
between devotion and the sacraments, a brief sampling of what
Thomas thinks about devotion in other contexts helps to set the stage.
For example, in the *prima secundae* when examining the ceremonial
precepts of the Old Law, Thomas says that devotion and obedience
constitute the justifying principles of the ceremonial precepts.[18]
Therefore, divine worship even according to the precepts of the Old
Law consists in a spiritual dimension characterized by "devotion of
the mind to God" and a corporeal dimension found in sacrifices and
oblations.[19] In addition, devotion of heart and desire contributed to
the establishment of the ceremonial precepts,[20] and thus are accorded
a certain degree of authority in the realm of ceremonial worship.
Nevertheless, the devotion exercised in the observance of the ceremonial precepts is what pleases God rather than the "things in
themselves."[21] In the *secunda secundae*, Thomas observes that the
relationship between faith and devotion is such that greater faith can
be attributed to those who possess greater devotion.[22] Therefore,
when Thomas explains the reasons why prayer to lesser saints may
prove more efficacious than prayer to more notable saints, he gives the

14. II-II, q. 82, a. 3, co.

15. II-II, q. 83, a. 15, co.

16. Cyprian Vagaggini, OSB, *Theological Dimensions of the Liturgy* (Collegeville, MN: The
Liturgical Press, 1976), 132.

17. See *Mediator Dei*, no. 32.

18. I-II, q. 100, a. 12, co.: "Hence it is said of these precepts that they did not justify man
save through the devotion and obedience of those who complied with them."

19. I-II, q. 102, a. 5, ad 4.

20. I-II, q. 103, a. 1, co.

21. I-II, q. 103, a. 2, ad 2.

22. II-II, q. 5, a. 4, co.: "Consequently a man's faith may be described as being greater, in one
way, on the part of his intellect, on account of its greater certitude and firmness, and, in another
way, on the part of his will, on account of his greater promptitude, devotion, or confidence."

credit to the greater devotion with which a lesser saint may be implored.[23] And those who do not avail themselves of ways to foster devotion in anticipation of prayer, risk tempting God and failing to prepare properly so as to be heard by God.[24] Lastly, when Thomas considers whether upon Christ's descent into hell all souls (other than the lost) were released, he answers that only those souls purified *sufficienter*, or those "who in life, by their faith and devotion towards Christ's death, so merited, that when He descended, they were delivered from the temporal punishment of Purgatory."[25]

It is, however, in Thomas's discussion of the sacraments, located in the *tertia pars*, that the role of devotion takes on the greatest significance. The reason for this is that Thomas links the fruitful communication of grace, both sacramental and sanctifying, to the quality of the interior dispositions of the recipient. In considering the first of the sacraments and the gateway to all the others, Thomas asks whether Baptism has an equal effect in all. His answer notes that insofar as it is the Church's faith that is considered, all children are equally disposed; but with respect to adults, all

> are not equally disposed, . . . for some approach thereto with greater, some with less, devotion. And therefore some receive a greater, some a smaller share of the grace of newness; just as from the same fire, he receives more heat who approaches nearest to it, although the fire, as far as it is concerned, sends forth its heat equally to all.[26]

In article 9 of question 69, Thomas specifically considers whether insincerity inhibits the effect of Baptism. Responding in the affirmative, he quotes Saint Augustine's teaching that lack of devotion is one of four possible ways in which one may be insincere and thus impede one's reception of the sacrament's effect (i.e., the grace of the sacrament).[27]

The connection between devotion and the effect of grace appears again in Thomas's treatment of the sacrament of the Eucharist. He begins by considering its elements and moves to a

23. II-II, q. 83, a. 11, ad 4.
24. II-II, q. 97, a. 3, ad 2.
25. III, q. 52, a. 8, ad 1.
26. III, q. 69, a. 8, co.
27. III, q. 69, a. 10, co.

consideration of its effects in question 79. Again, devotion on the part
of the recipient is directly linked to fruitful reception of the effect of
the sacrament. The principal effect of the sacrament of the Eucharist
is union with Christ in charity. From this union flow other related
effects, such as an increase of grace, spiritual nourishment, forgiveness
of venial sins, forgiveness of guilt and the punishment of sin, preser-
vation from future sin by being strengthened, the perfection of the
spiritual life, and attainment of glory.[28] But, Thomas notes, "It sometimes happens that a man is hindered from receiving the effect of
this sacrament."[29] The only specific discussion about an absolute
barrier to receiving the effect of this sacrament concerns the obstacle
of mortal sin—the condition in which man is spiritually dead and
incapable of being united with Christ, which union is the intended
effect of the sacrament.[30] But there are lesser barriers to receiving the
full fruits of the sacrament, of which the chief obstacle is lack of
devotion. Article 3 of question 79 provides a very clear example of
the significance of devotion and its effect on the benefits of both the
sacramental and the sacrificial dimensions of the Eucharist. The
question concerns the sacrament's effect with respect to forgiveness of
the punishment due to sin. Thomas first points out that the Eucharist
is both a sacrifice and a sacrament. It is a sacrifice insofar as it is
offered up and it is a sacrament insofar as it is received.[31] The effect of
the sacrament flows to the recipient, whereas the effect of the sacrifice
flows to the offerer or those for whom the sacrifice is made. With
respect to the sacramental dimension of the Eucharist, sin is forgiven
only "according to the measure of [man's] devotion and fervor."
Similarly, when considering the Eucharist as sacrifice, it "suffices of its
own quantity to satisfy for all punishment [because it is Christ who
has made the sacrifice], yet it becomes satisfactory for them for whom
it is offered, or even for the offerers, according to the measure of
their devotion, and not for the whole punishment."[32] Finally, in
response to an objector who asserts that the whole of punishment due
to sin must be remitted because Christ's infinite power is contained

---

28. III, q. 79.
29. III, q. 80 a. 1, co.
30. III, q. 79 a. 3.
31. III, q. 79, a. 5, co.
32. III, q. 79, a. 5, co.

in the sacrament, Thomas's reply is unequivocal: "If part of the punishment and not the whole be taken away by this sacrament, it is due to a defect not on the part of Christ's power, but on the part of man's devotion."[33]

The role of devotion is also considered by Thomas in other contexts involving the Eucharist, such as when he takes into account the role of the minister of the sacrament in question 82. He affirms that the devotion of the priest determines the efficacy of the prayers offered by him, and that in this respect there is "no doubt but that the mass of the better priest is the more fruitful."[34] Even the requirement that children attain the age of reason prior to receiving Holy Communion rests on the fact that reason gives rise to devotion,[35] although Thomas says that there are cases in which those who lack adequate reason possess sufficient devotion and thus are permitted to receive the sacrament.[36] Finally, in his examination of the questions concerning the use of the sacrament, he considers whether it is lawful to receive Holy Communion daily. In typical fashion, Thomas says there are two things to be considered regarding the use of the sacrament; first, the great benefit received which makes it profitable to receive daily, and second the recipient's need for "great reverence and devotion."[37] Accordingly, he says that receiving Holy Communion calls for "*maxima devotio*" because it is at the moment of reception that the effect of the sacrament is received.[38] With respect to celebrating the sacrament of the Eucharist, he states that benefits flow to members of the Church (whether or not they receive Holy Communion) "more or less, according to the measure of their devotion."[39]

33. III, q. 79, a. 5, ad 3.

34. III, q. 82, a. 6, co.

35. III, q. 80, a. 9, ad 3: "But when children once begin to have some use of reason so as to be able to conceive some devotion for the sacrament, then it can be given to them."

36. III, q. 80, a. 9, ad 1: "Those lacking the use of reason can have devotion towards the sacrament; actual devotion in some cases, and past in others."

37. III, q. 80, a. 10, co.

38. III, q. 80, a. 8, ad 6.

39. III, q. 79, a. 7, ad 2.

The Connection Between *Devotio* and *Solemnitas*

What does Thomas say regarding how to bring about devotion? In the first instance he acknowledges that the extrinsic and principal cause of devotion is God who calls whom he wills as he wills.[40] On our part, however, the principal intrinsic cause of devotion is meditation or contemplation, because devotion is an act of the will in which man surrenders himself readily to the service of God, and all acts of the will arise from some consideration.[41] What are the external causes on our part? Thomas notes that things such as the practice of offering sacrifice and gifts,[42] praying in a consecrated place,[43] and the use of consecrated things for divine service all foster devotion.[44] Use of our bodies to exhibit humility incites our affections and leads to interior devotion.[45] The use of the voice in prayer "excites interior devotion" and "raises the mind to God."[46] The prayers offered during Mass, in particular the Preface, are intended to "excite devotion."[47] Devotion is also aroused by offering praise to God by speech and song,[48] as well as by fasting,[49] and it is strengthened by taking a vow, especially the vows made in religious profession.[50] On this topic he quotes Saint Augustine who remarks that our prayers need to be frequent "lest devotion be extinguished as soon as it is kindled."[51] Yet of all the means for cultivating devotion, Thomas most frequently mentions a certain solemnity.

He uses the term principally in two ways: in one way, with reference to a "certain solemnity" specifically for the purpose of fostering devotion and, in the other, with reference to a "certain

---

40. II-II, q. 82, a. 3, co.
41. Ibid.
42. II-II, q. 30, a. 4, ad 1.
43. II-II, q. 84, a. 3, ad 2.
44. III, q. 83, a. 3, ad 3.
45. II-II, q. 84, a. 2, co.
46. II-II, q. 83, a. 12, co.
47. III, q. 83, a. 4.
48. II-II, q. 91, aa. 1 and 2.
49. II-II, q. 147, a. 5, co.
50. II-II, q. 88, a. 6, ad 1.
51. II-II, q. 171, a. 2, ad 2.

solemnity" necessary to the importance of the occasion (that is, in the Old Law for the annual celebration of certain feasts as well as the weekly celebration of the Sabbath and, in the New Law, celebration of the Mass and the other sacraments, episcopal ordination, profession of religious vows,[52] taking of oaths, and consecration of a church building).[53] The different uses of the term do not necessarily operate in isolation from each other, for the solemnity that gives rise to devotion also ought to be fitting for the occasion, just as the solemnity suited to the event ought to assist in fostering the appropriate disposition of heart and mind called for by the seriousness of the event. In both instances, solemnity is an external means to foster the interior dispositions necessary for both the fruitful reception of grace and fitting worship.

It is in connection with Thomas's examination of the various sacramental rites of the Church, particularly Baptism and the Eucharist, that solemnity is given a specific form. However, the general framework for examining and discussing the meaning of solemnity and its role in the liturgy is provided in question 64, article 2, when Thomas distinguishes what is and is not essential to the sacraments. When an objector claims that God must not be the cause of the sacraments because there are things in the celebration of the sacraments that are not of divine origin, Thomas replies, "Human institutions observed in the sacraments are not essential to the sacrament; but belong to the solemnity which is added to the sacraments in order to arouse devotion and reverence in the recipients."[54] He makes very clear that human institutions are added to the sacraments because men need help in arousing proper devotion and reverence; nonetheless, these aids are not essential to the sacrament itself. He makes this point several times in his examination of the sacrament of Baptism, and especially in his discussion of the rite of Baptism in question 66. The distinction is first made in the *respondeo* when Thomas states that there are things done in the rite that are essential to the sacrament and things that are not essential. The essential elements consist in the

---

52. II-II, q. 184, aa. 4 and 5.

53. III, q. 83, a. 3.

54. III, q. 64, a. 2, ad 1: "illa quae aguntur in sacramentis per homines instituta, non sunt de necessitate sacramenti, sed ad quandam solemnitatem, quae adhibetur sacramentis ad excitandam devotionem et reverentiam in his qui sacramenta suscipiunt."

form, the matter, and the minister, but "all the other things which
the Church observes in the baptismal rite belong rather to a certain
solemnity of the sacrament."[55] He goes on to state that these "other
things" are used in conjunction with the sacrament to serve three
purposes: to arouse devotion, to instruct the faithful, and to restrain
the power of the devil. It is most instructive to note that when
Thomas elaborates on the first purpose of fostering devotion, he adds,
"For if there were nothing done but a mere washing with water,
without any solemnity, some might easily think it to be an ordinary
washing."[56] The comment seems quite pertinent today given the
modern tendency to celebrate the liturgy of the sacraments too casually.
In any event, the "other things" to which objections are raised include
the use of chrism oil as well as the anointing three times with the
oil; first the breast is anointed so as to symbolize reception of the Holy
Spirit, next the shoulders are anointed to represent the clothing with
grace that is conferred by the sacrament, and finally, the head is
anointed while the priest offers a prayer that the newly baptized might
have a share in Christ's kingdom and be called by the name of
Christian. An additional objection is raised concerning the use of a
blessing for the water. The argument here is that if water were the
proper matter, it would require no blessing. Thomas replies that water
is the proper matter according to the words of Christ, whereas the
blessing, though not essential to the sacrament, "belongs to a certain
solemnity, whereby the devotion of the faithful is aroused."[57] Finally,
Thomas rejects the charge that these and other non-essential
aspects have been "unsuitably inserted" into the rite and are superfluous because, after all, the sacrament can be celebrated without
them. He notes that they are far from superfluous because they
belong to the solemnity of the sacrament and as such "pertain to the
sacrament's well-being."[58]

Question 83 of the *tertia pars* is the last of the 11 questions in
which Thomas examines the Eucharist. At this point in the *Summa*

---

55. III, q. 66, a. 10, co.

56. Ibid.: "Primo quidem, ad excitandam devotionem fidelium, et reverentiam ad
sacramentum. Si enim simpliciter fieret ablutio in aqua, absque solemnitate, de facili ab aliquibus
aestimaretur quasi quaedam communis ablutio."

57. III, q. 66, a. 3, ad 5.

58. III, q. 66, a.10, obj. 4: "Haec igitur quae dicta sunt, videntur esse superflua, et ita
inconvenienter ab Ecclesia instituta esse in ritu Baptismi."

he has already thoroughly examined what is essential to the sacrament. In questions 73 through 82, he has looked at the form, the matter, the effects, the miracle of transubstantiation, the way in which Christ is present in the sacrament, the accidents, the use of the sacrament in general, the use that Christ made of the sacrament at its institution, and the minister of the sacrament. Finally, in question 83, he considers the rite of the sacrament, that is, the Mass in its non-essential elements insofar as confecting the sacrament is concerned. With the exception of the first and sixth articles, the other four articles in question 83 are framed almost entirely in terms of objections aimed at solemnity in one of its forms. Whether for the proper celebration of the sacrament and fitting worship or for what is conducive to cultivating devotion, both aspects can be said to apply to proper worship as well as an increase of devotion. It is through examination of the objections (which have a remarkably modern ring to them) and Thomas's responses to them that we can discern what he means when he speaks about human institutions pertaining to solemnity that are added to the sacraments. For example, article 3 considers such things as whether Mass should be celebrated in a church building set aside and consecrated for that purpose; whether Mass should be celebrated using sacred vessels made of precious metals and consecrated for that purpose; whether the altar should be consecrated; and whether only linen should be used for altar cloths. As in the preceding article, two things are considered regarding the equipment: "one of these belongs to the representation of the events connected with our Lord's Passion; while the other is connected with the reverence due to the sacrament, in which Christ is contained verily, and not in figure only."[59] In each instance, Thomas builds his case on the basis of what is fitting for divine worship or what leads to devotion on the part of those who will receive the sacrament.

It is in response to the question in article 4 ("whether the words spoken in this sacrament are properly framed") that we are given a detailed description of the order and content of the Mass as it was celebrated in Thomas's age. As the question's title suggests, the objections focus on the words used during Mass, and their main thrust is that the words used (other than those of institution) were not

---

59. III, q. 83, a. 3, co.

used by Christ and cannot be found in the Gospel, and therefore they should not be used in the sacrament. Additional objections include the views that prayers should not be offered for the salvation of the faithful, because in the celebration of the other sacraments such prayers are not offered, and that neither other ministers nor the choir nor the faithful should speak during the celebration, because the priest is the sole minister of the sacrament. Thomas responds individually to each objection. But what is most telling for our purposes is that he commences his *respondeo* by implicitly identifying all of the contested parts of the Mass as belonging to the order of solemnity: "Since the whole mystery of our salvation is comprised in this sacrament, therefore is it performed with greater solemnity than the other sacraments."[60] This is the foundation upon which he begins to address these objections. In his response he organizes the Mass into four parts: preparation, instruction, consecration, and thanksgiving. The preparation, instruction, and thanksgiving, as well as significant portions of the consecration, all involve words fashioned for the purpose of fitting worship and preparation of the mind and heart to participate in the great mystery. Thomas's reply to the first of the objections states that the "consecration is accomplished by Christ's words only," but "the other words must be added to dispose the people for receiving it." These "other words" include the Gloria, the Sanctus, the Creed, all of the prayers offered by the priest (such as the prayers for worthy celebration of the sacrament), prayers for the dead, prayers to the saints, and prayers for the salvation of the whole people, the singing of the Alleluia, and the reading of the Gospel. In the fifth objection, the argument against the "additional words" is based on an implicit acknowledgment that such words succeed quite well in fostering devotion. The objector reasons that the additional words stir up devotion, but that the Eucharist does not require greater devotion. Thomas responds by saying that because the whole Christ is contained in the sacrament of the Eucharist, it is deserving of greater devotion. He goes on to add that the Eucharist is also worthy of a greater general devotion on the part of the people because it is offered for the whole people and not just for the recipients of the sacrament.

---

60. III, q. 83, a. 4, co.

After looking at the overall structure of the rite through its words, 12 objections are raised in article 5 concerning the actions done by the priest during celebration of the Mass. These actions include using incense, repeating the Sign of the Cross, stretching out the arms, joining the hands, joining the fingers, bowing, turning to face the people, and greeting the people. Other objections concern the breaking of the host, reservation of the host, mixing of a particle of Christ's Body with his Blood, and celebration of Mass with only one server. In the *respondeo* Thomas's reply is consistent with his reasoning in article 4. These actions serve one or all of the following purposes: "some things are done in order to represent Christ's Passion, or the disposing of His mystical body, and some others are done which pertain to the devotion and reverence due to this sacrament." Almost all of the non-essential parts in the celebration of the Eucharist described above belong to a certain solemnity that is incorporated into the rite for the purpose of the devotion and reverence due the sacrament.

HUMAN NATURE NEEDS *SOLEMNITAS*

Human nature needs solemnity. According to John Paul II this should not surprise us. In his apostolic letter *Rosarium Virginis Mariae*, he writes:

> God communicates himself to us respecting our human nature and its vital rhythms. Hence, while Christian spirituality is familiar with the most sublime forms of mystical silence in which images, words and gestures are all, so to speak, superseded by an intense and ineffable union with God, it normally engages the whole person in all his complex psychological, physical and relational reality. This becomes apparent in the Liturgy. Sacraments and sacramentals are structured as a series of rites which bring into play all the dimensions of the person.[61]

Likewise, Thomas's recognition of the need for a certain solemnity in order to arouse devotion is rooted in his understanding of human nature. Four basic truths concerning human nature that indelibly mark all of Thomas's thought also provide the underpinning for his persistent assertion that solemnity is necessary to man in the celebration of the sacraments. The first truth is that man "is ordained

---

61. *Rosarium Virginis Mariae*, no. 27.

by the Divine Providence to a higher good than human fragility can experience in this present life."[62] Man is called to something higher than his reason can reach here and now, and so he must learn to direct his desire toward the divine good. This will prepare him for his destiny beyond time.[63] Knowledge of his true end, union with God in the beatific vision, exceeds man's powers of comprehension, and so this truth must be placed before him in order that he may learn to desire it. It is due to this weakness in human nature that solemnity in the celebration of the sacraments, and especially in the Liturgy of the Eucharist, is so essential. Man needs "a guiding hand, not only to the knowledge, but also to the love of Divine things by means of certain sensible objects [so that he] may be caught up to the love of things invisible."[64] Solemnity proposes to man through his senses that which transcends human reason[65] and points to the sacred, that which is "deputed to the divine worship."[66] It reinforces our fragile faith by reminding us of things divine and thereby elevating our earthbound dispositions. It is thus that a certain solemnity, by orienting us toward the mystery of the transcendent, arouses in us the desire for our true end and leads to devotion.

The second truth about human nature pertinent to our discussion is that man is a creature who in justice owes worship to his creator.[67] The virtue of religion of which devotion is the principal act presupposes this aspect of human nature. The third truth concerns man's constitution as a creature made up of body and soul. Accordingly, man must worship his creator with both body and soul—the soul by an interior worship and the body by an outward worship, in which the outward worship is ordained to the internal worship.[68] Man worships God interiorly by reverence, which consists in dispositions of admiration, esteem, honor, entreaty, humility, submission,

---

62. *Summa Contra Gentiles* I, 5, § 2. For quotations from the *Summa Contra Gentiles*, I have used the translations by Anton C. Pegis for Book One: God, and Charles J. O'Neill for Book Four: Salvation (Saint Thomas Aquinas, *Summa Contra Gentiles*, 5 vols.) (Notre Dame: University of Notre Dame Press, 1975).

63. Anton Pegis, "General Introduction" in *Summa Contra Gentiles*, Book One: God, 29–30.

64. II-II, q. 82, a. 3, ad 2.

65. SCG I, 5, § 2.

66. II-II, q. 99, a. 1, co.

67. See II-II, q. 81, aa. 4 and 5.

68. I-II, q. 101, a. 2; II-II, q. 81, a. 7, co.

and repentance.[69] Externally he worships God with physical expressions that exhibit honor, humility, and submission.[70] The characteristics of solemnity in the liturgy not only foster these interior dispositions, but also incorporate the external manifestations appropriate to fitting worship. In addition, man's constitution involves an interdependence between body and soul that is manifested in a pervasive relationship between his external acts and his internal disposition. What we perceive with our senses and do with our bodies shapes our interior; conversely, the state of our mind and heart is reflected in our actions. Solemnity consists in external practices that not only incite man's devotion and reverence, but also express man's response to the pre-eminence of God in his midst.

The fourth point to be considered is the notion originating with Aristotle that man receives all knowledge through his senses. Accordingly, he is led not only to material but also to spiritual and intelligible reality through his senses.[71] Thomas tells us that with respect to "Divine worship it is necessary to make use of corporeal things, that man's mind may be aroused thereby, as by signs, to the spiritual acts by means of which he is united to God."[72] Signs speak to us through our senses, and God has provided for us reminders of divine things in the order of sensible objects. To this end sacraments are also (but not exclusively) signs.[73] The role and importance of signs as well as their relationship to the sacraments has been the topic of extensive consideration over the years, and so this chapter will leave that matter to more competent minds.[74] However, signs are integral to solemnity. In the liturgy they act as external expressions of the invisible and are a means to excite devotion and fervor in the heart and serve to engage, remind, and reorient the mind toward God.

---

69. Vagaggini, *Theological Dimensions of the Liturgy*, 70.

70. II-II, q. 84, a. 2, co.

71. SCG IV, ch. 56, par. 3.

72. II-II, q. 81 a. 7, co.

73. SCG III, ch. 119, par. 1.

74. It is hardly possible to give even a representative sampling of those examinations; however, for a recent consideration of the topic see John Yocum, "Sacraments in Aquinas," in *Aquinas on Doctrine: A Critical Introduction*, eds. Thomas Weinandy, Daniel Keating and John Yocum (New York: T. & T. Clark, 2004), and for a listing of some recent considerations of Saint Thomas's sacramental theology see Nathan Lefler, "Sign, Cause, and Person in St. Thomas's Sacramental Theology: Further Considerations," *Nova et Vetera* 4 (2006): 381–2 note 1.

In this connection a powerful reminder of our great need for solemnity is presented when Thomas considers in question 30 of the *tertia pars* whether it was fitting for the angel of the Annunciation to appear in a bodily vision to the Blessed Virgin Mary. He answers in the affirmative and, in typical fashion, gives three reasons why the apparition was indeed fitting. He first comments that the announcement of the Incarnation of the invisible God is rightly made by an invisible herald made visible. He next considers it fitting because the Incarnation was to take place in both the mind and the body of the Mother of God, and therefore "it behooved not only her mind, but also her bodily senses to be refreshed by the angelic vision." Finally, he adverts to the limits of human nature by acknowledging that "we apprehend with greater certainty that which is before our eyes, than what is in our imagination." He completes his reply by quoting Saint John Chrysostom: "For since [the Blessed Virgin] was receiving from the angel a message exceeding great, before such an event she needed a vision of *great solemnity*."[75] For fallen mankind, the implications of this statement are potent indeed. The Blessed Virgin Mary was the most perfect of all God's creatures, full of grace and endowed with a human nature preserved from every defect. If the Mother of God was in need of "a vision of great solemnity" in order to receive the message of the angel, it is surely reasonable to conclude that we, sharing the same nature but blinded by sin and hard of heart, are in need of solemnity in the liturgy to a very great degree indeed, that is, in some measure proportioned to our falleness.

What Is *Solemnitas*?

It is here that the thorniest issue presents itself. It seems clear that solemnity must hold a privileged place in the Church's consideration of the liturgy because of its indisputable role in the cultivation of devotion. This is especially true during the celebration of the Eucharist, the "source and summit of the whole of Christian life"[76] and the locus

---

75. III, q. 30, a. 3, co.

76. *Redemptionis Sacramentum*, preamble, no. 2; cf. *Lumen Gentium* no. 11: "fount and apex" (Vatican translation).

of man's deification,[77] which nonetheless is always ordered to the glorification of God.[78] Yet, what exactly constitutes a certain solemnity in the liturgy?

From our examination of Thomas's thought we can draw several conclusions. First, solemnity is made up of human institutions added to the celebration of the sacraments principally for the purpose of cultivating a spirit of devotion in those who participate in the liturgical celebration.[79] Second, solemnity is necessitated by, and in large measure is determined by, various aspects of human nature, including union with God as the proper end of man, the constitution of man as a body-soul composite, and the weakness of human nature due to original sin. Third, solemnity mostly involves things external to man, even though man's interior disposition ought to contribute to the overall integrity of an attitude and atmosphere of solemnity. Fourth, solemnity must take a form that possesses a correspondence to the invisible reality occurring in the sacrament being celebrated, above all in the case of the sacrament of the Eucharist. Therefore, solemnity must evoke a certain *gravitas*, a dignity that aspires to reflect and respond to the magnitude of the divine act occurring in our midst. Such orientation to the transcendent necessarily implies acknowledgment of a great mystery and points to the sacred, to what is holy. This fourth characteristic (which is dependent upon and cannot be properly understood apart from the others) seems to provoke the most controversy, both by the insistence of its presence and by the fact that it must take a particular form; that is, it must conform to the invisible, unchanging reality occurring in the sacrament, and as such, it may not be readily altered according to inclination.

Josef Pieper has written about the desacralizing tendencies of modernity and the consequent impact on the Church's liturgy.[80] Considering some characteristics of the sacred proposed by Pieper will help to flesh out the essence of solemnity and especially the last

---

77. Matthew Levering, "The Liturgy of the Eucharist," in *Aquinas on Doctrine: A Critical Introduction*, eds. Thomas Weinandy, Daniel Keating and John Yocum (New York: T. & T. Clark, 2004), 183.

78. Berger, *Thomas Aquinas and the Liturgy*, quoting Cyprian Vagaggini, 87.

79. Additional, though secondary, purposes of solemnity in the sacraments include instruction of the faithful and restraining the devil. Cf. III, q. 66, a. 10, co.

80. See Pieper, *In Search of the Sacred*.

characteristic.[81] At the outset he quotes Thomas in defining something as sacred because of its relation to the act of public worship.[82] He then notes that the sacred is what is set apart from the common routine of daily life.[83] Opponents of this view insist that the sacred must be incorporated into daily life and argue against such separation by reasoning that it is contrary to what is truly human. Pieper rightly observes that such arguments rest "on a deplorable misconception" of the true nature of man "who in essence refuses to be 'merely human' " because man's true end is his divinization. Next, Pieper identifies what he calls "sacred language," a term that includes gestures, signs, and words.[84] Many of the things that Thomas identifies as belonging to solemnity come within Pieper's meaning of "sacred language": for example, blessings; prayers; the use of incense; wearing of special garments either by the recipient of the sacrament or by the priests; consecration of structures (altars, sacred vessels made of precious metals); bodily gestures, including folding hands, outstretched arms, bowing, kneeling and prostration, singing, anointing with oil; and lastly, the celebration of the sacraments in a church building that is set apart and consecrated for such purpose alone. Thomas does not mention specifically the orientation of liturgical prayer facing east or the use of Latin, but it is safe to say that if presented with these questions today, he would attribute both to a certain solemnity.[85]

---

81. See also *Mediator Dei*, no. 188, in which Pope Pius XII says that three characteristics "should adorn all liturgical services: sacredness, which abhors any profane influence; nobility, which true and genuine arts should serve and foster; and universality, which while safeguarding local and legitimate custom, reveals the Catholic unity of the Church."

82. Pieper, *In Search of the Sacred*, 25.

83. Ibid., 32.

84. Ibid., 41.

85. Additional clues as to what Thomas means by *solemnitas* can be found in question 184 of the *secunda secundae* concerning the state of perfection. In articles 4, 5, and 6, he discusses solemnity in connection with religious profession and episcopal ordination. He teaches that "there is required for the state of perfection a perpetual obligation to things pertaining to perfection, together with a certain solemnity." He pairs solemnity with consecration and profession of vows and comments that men normally observe a certain solemnity in connection with things having to do with perpetuity. His use of solemnity comes very close to meaning consecration in some places within the question, but its precise meaning remains somewhat vague. In any case, it appears to be more than an essential psychological feature as it is referred to as one of two requirements for the state of perfection. This is in contrast to the clear assertion that those things pertaining to a certain solemnity are not essential with respect to the sacraments of Baptism and the Eucharist, but are nevertheless necessary for the faithful.

It is precisely what Pieper calls the "strict formality"[86] of all sacred language that is a particularly defining characteristic of solemnity and cannot be understood (or defended) apart from the concept of the sacred. He compares the necessity and permanent character of the form of sacred language to an inherent quality not unlike that of a finished poem that may not be altered on a whim. This notion also appears in the writings of Pope Benedict XVI, in his concept of "unspontaneity": "The greatness of the liturgy depends . . . on its unspontaneity."[87] In other words, the greatness of the liturgy depends on the strict formality of the sacred language, which constitutes in large measure that which Thomas refers to as a certain solemnity. According to the Holy Father, creativity "cannot be an authentic category for matters liturgical"[88] because liturgy is not manufactured but is "characterized by adherence to the form of faith that has developed in the apostolic Tradition." Furthermore, as Liam Walsh, OP, has pointed out, according to Thomas everything that prepares man for grace and enables him to act in conformity with it is itself a product of God's grace. Therefore, "the full liturgical celebration of sacraments is the work of God, not as the product of divine law but as the product of divine grace."[89] Ultimately, "the life of the liturgy does not come from what dawns upon the minds of individuals . . . but is God's descent upon our world."[90] This understanding of liturgy is the foundation that gives rise to an attentiveness to the mystery, transcendence, and sacredness that at once responds to and calls forth a certain solemnity.

Even though neither Thomas nor Pieper elaborate upon it explicitly, silence is an element of solemnity that is essential to the discussion. Thomas implicitly refers to silence in question 83, article 4 when he distinguishes those prayers common to both the priest and

---

86. Pieper, *In Search of the Sacred*, 41.

87. Joseph Cardinal Ratzinger, *The Spirit of the Liturgy*, trans. John Saward (San Francisco: Ignatius Press, 2000), 166.

88. Ratzinger, *The Spirit of the Liturgy*, 168. This statement by the Holy Father seems to be somewhat in tension with paragraph 39 of *Redemptionis Sacramentum*, which states in part: "ample flexibility is given for appropriate creativity aimed at allowing each celebration to be adapted to the needs of the participants, to their comprehension, their interior preparation and their gifts, according to the established liturgical norms."

89. Walsh, "Liturgy in the Theology of St. Thomas," 580.

90. Ratzinger, *The Spirit of the Liturgy*, 168.

the faithful from the prayers belonging to the priest alone, which must be said in secret.[91] From this we can conclude that periods of silence are meant to be a constituent part of the liturgy. Pope Benedict XVI has expressed strong views on the need for silence in his book *The Spirit of the Liturgy*, written before he was elected Pope. He discusses silence in a subchapter titled "The Human Voice."[92] While I do not think this title was meant to be ironic, it is telling that the bulk of his examination of the role of the human voice in the liturgy is taken up with reflections on the integral part of silence and its neglect in the present form of the liturgy. Like Thomas, he too mentions the silent prayers of the priest, though greatly reduced in number and, to my mind, almost indistinguishable within the liturgy of today. He also asserts that it is not true that recitation aloud of the whole Eucharistic Prayer is necessary for the full participation in the Mass of all present. He writes persuasively of the experience of a "content-filled" silence that gives us "a positive stillness" that restores us. When all are united in the silent praying of the Canon and the "recollection and devotion" with which the praying priest shows forth the "dignity and grandeur of the Gospel," the faithful are helped to "understand how tremendous" is the word of God in their midst:

> This silence is not just a period of waiting, something external. . . . something happens inwardly that corresponds to what is going on outwardly—we are disposing ourselves, preparing the way, placing ourselves before the Lord, asking him to make us ready for transformation. Shared silence becomes shared prayer, indeed shared action, a journey out of our everyday life toward the Lord, toward merging our time with his own.[93]

Here, in a few sentences about silence, we see mentioned many of the elements that have been considered with respect to solemnity. Here we also see evidence of the authentic communion that gives rise to community,[94] the ubiquitous term that has dominated the discussion concerning the reform of the liturgy almost to the same degree that has the call for "active participation." In this connection it seems to

---

91. III, q. 83, a. 4, ad 6.

92. See Ratzinger, *The Spirit of the Liturgy*, 207–16. See also Joseph Cardinal Ratzinger, *Feast of Faith* (San Francisco: Ignatius Press, 1981) 61–75, for additional considerations on the structure of the liturgy.

93. Ratzinger, *The Spirit of the Liturgy*, 211.

94. See Ratzinger, *Feast of Faith*, 68–75, for more reflections on community and the liturgy.

me that most of the disagreements about the liturgy since the imple-
mentation of the reform initiated by the Second Vatican Council
concern solemnity in one way or another, either explicitly concerning
the fourth characteristic discussed or implicitly with regard to the
first three. Whether the arguments assert too much, not enough, or a
wholly new understanding of the shape that solemnity in the liturgy
should take, the question of a certain solemnity in the liturgy has been
at the heart of almost all of the controversy.

CONCLUSION

This brings us to the end of our considerations on the role of *solemni-*
tas in the liturgy. The passages I quoted at the beginning of this essay
were meant to bring to mind two considerations: 1) the terrible and
awesome God to whom we owe our homage and worship, and 2) the
miracle of transformation brought about in the human soul through
the sanctifying effects of the Eucharist. In this life, we can only
approximate the dispositions appropriate to such awesome mysteries.
Yet Thomas has provided us with a framework for making our best
efforts to do so through the external means he calls *solemnitas*.

   If there is a certain emptiness in much of the modern liturgy,
despite its conformity in many respects with Thomas's description of
the rite in question 83 of the *tertia pars*, I suggest that it is due in large
measure to the lack of solemnity in the liturgy and the consequent
weakness of faith and devotion. It is solemnity in the liturgy that is
the bulwark of both faith and devotion, in the presence of the wholly
invisible miracle of transubstantiation.[95] When our minds are taken
up by trivial distractions and the hoped-for contemplation of higher
things eludes us—or when the burdens of this life, likened to a
long night in a bad inn by Saint Teresa of Avila, overwhelm us and
prevent us from making way for the *actio divina*—it is then most
of all that we need solemnity. We need solemnity to be a guiding hand
and a stronghold that provides a concrete reminder of what is happen-
ing and why we have come in the first place. And yet, even under
the best of circumstances (and I cannot help but think of our daily
conventual Mass) the fire of devotion still needs to be fed because of

---

95. See Peter A. Kwasniewski, "St. Thomas and the Ecstatic Practice of Theology," in *Nova et*
Vetera 2 (2004): 85, note 80, quoting Charles DeKoninck.

our fallen human nature. It is in this regard that Pope Benedict XVI has been compelled to say: "One of man's deepest needs . . . is manifestly not being met in our present form of the liturgy."[96]

If modern sensibilities seem to be unresponsive to the characteristics of solemnity that we have examined, it is only further evidence of the increasing alienation of modern man from his own true nature. Human nature has not changed since the time of Saint Thomas, and the need for solemnity in the liturgy, as well as its particular characteristics and form, is firmly rooted in human nature. In connection with the form of the liturgy, Pope Benedict has remarked, "In the interplay between culture and history, history has priority."[97] A similar claim may be made with respect to the priority of the truths concerning human nature. In an age of increasing unbelief, now is not the time to accommodate claims to the contrary, but rather it is the time to reawaken man to himself and to God through the explicit, even if shocking, return of solemnity to the liturgy. Human nature will respond if solemnity is authentically and integrally present in the liturgy. In this, as in so many things, Saint Thomas proves to be a trustworthy guide.

96. Ratzinger, *The Spirit of the Liturgy*, 209.
97. Ibid., 224.

English-Language Resources for Further Study

Berger, David. *Thomas Aquinas and the Liturgy*, translated by Christopher Grosz. Ypsilanti, MI: Sapientia Press, 2004.

Blankenhorn, Bernhard, OP. "The Instrumental Causality of the Sacraments: Thomas Aquinas and Louis-Marie Chauvet." *Nova et Vetera* 4 (2006): 255–94.

Brock, Stephen L. "St. Thomas and Eucharistic Conversion." *The Thomist* 65 (2001): 529–65.

Cessario, Romanus, OP. "The Sacramental Mediation of Divine Friendship and Communion." *Faith and Reason* 27 (2002): 7–41.

———. "'Circa res . . . aliquid fit' (*Summa Theologiae* II-II, q. 85, a. 3, ad 3): Aquinas on New Law Sacrifice." *Nova et Vetera* 4 (2006): 295–312.

Dauphinais, Michael. "'And they shall all be taught by God': Wisdom and the Eucharist in John 6." In *Reading John with St. Thomas Aquinas*, Michael Dauphinais and Matthew Levering, editors, 312–7. Washington, DC: The Catholic University of America Press, 2005.

Dulles, Avery, SJ. "The Eucharist as Sacrifice." In *Rediscovering the Eucharist: Ecumenical Conversations*, Roch Kereszty, OCIST, editor, 175–87. New York: Paulist Press, 2003.

Emery, Gilles, OP. "The Ecclesial Fruit of the Eucharist in St. Thomas Aquinas," translated by Therese C. Scarpelli. *Nova et Vetera* 2 (2004): 43–60.

Levering, Matthew. *Sacrifice and Community: Jewish Offering and Christian Eucharist*. Oxford: Blackwell, 2005.

McCabe, Herbert, OP. "Sacramental Language." In idem, *God Matters*, 165–79. London: Mowbray, 1987.

O'Neill, Colman, OP. *Sacramental Realism: A General Theory of the Sacraments*. Chicago: Midwest Theological Forum, 1998.

———. *Meeting Christ in the Sacraments*, edited by Romanus Cessario, OP. New York: Alba House, 1991.

———. "The Mysteries of Christ and the Sacraments." *The Thomist* 25 (1962): 1–53.

———. "St. Thomas on the Membership of the Church." *The Thomist* 27 (1963): 88–140.

Vonier, Abbot Anscar, OSB. *A Key to the Doctrine of the Eucharist*. Bethesda, MD: Zaccheus Press, 2003.

Walsh, Liam, OP. "The Divine and the Human in St. Thomas's Theology of the Sacraments." In *Ordo sapientiae et amoris*, edited by C.-J. Pinto de Oliveira, OP, 321–52. Fribourg: Éditions universitaires, 1993.

———. "Liturgy in the Theology of St. Thomas." *The Thomist* 38 (1974): 557–83.

———. *The Sacraments of Initiation*. London: Geoffrey Chapman, 1988.

Yocum, John. "Sacraments in Aquinas." In *Aquinas on Doctrine: A Critical Introduction*, edited by Thomas Weinandy, OFM CAP, Daniel Keating, and John Yocum, 159–81. Edinburgh: T. & T. Clark, 2004.

Name Index

Contributors

Sister Thomas Augustine Becker, OP, is a member of the Dominican Sisters of Mary, Mother of the Eucharist, located in Ann Arbor, Michigan. She earned her JD from St. John's University, New York, and her BM from Berklee College of Music, Boston. Prior to entering religious life she practiced law in New York City. She is presently earning an MA in Educational Administration and plans to go on for further study in canon law.

John F. Boyle is Professor of Catholic Studies and Theology at the University of St. Thomas in St. Paul, Minnesota, where he has taught since earning his PHD in Medieval Studies from the Center for Medieval Studies at the University of Toronto. In 1995 he was named University of St. Thomas Distinguished Educator of the Year. In addition to numerous articles in scholarly volumes and such journals as *The Thomist* and *Pro Ecclesia*, he has recently published with the late Leonard Boyle, OP, a critical Latin edition of Thomas Aquinas's second commentary on Book I of the *Liber Sententiarum* of Peter Lombard.

Romanus Cessario, OP, is Professor of Systematic Theology at St. John's Seminary in Brighton, Massachusetts, and also taught for many years at the Dominican House of Studies in Washington, DC. In addition to many scholarly and popular articles, he has written many books, including *A Short History of Thomism* (originally published in French as *Le thomisme et les thomistes*), *Introduction to Moral Theology, Christian Faith and the Theological Life, The Moral Virtues and Theological Ethics*, and *The Godly Image*. He co-edited *Veritatis Splendor and the Renewal of Moral Theology*. He edits series in moral theology for both Fordham University Press and The Catholic University of America Press, and serves as associate editor of *The Thomist* and as senior editor of *Magnificat*.

Michael Dauphinais is Dean of Faculty and Associate Professor of Theology at Ave Maria University. He previously taught theology at the University of St. Thomas in St. Paul, Minnesota. In addition to his administrative responsibilities, he is the co-director of the Aquinas Center for Theological Renewal and co-editor of *Nova et Vetera*. Together with Matthew Levering, he co-authored *Holy People, Holy Land: A Theological Introduction to the Bible* and *Knowing the Love of Christ: An Introduction to the Theology of St. Thomas Aquinas*, and co-edited *Reading John with St. Thomas Aquinas* and *John Paul II and St. Thomas Aquinas*. With Barry David and Matthew Levering, he co-edited *Aquinas the Augustinian*. He has published articles in *The Thomist* and *Nova et Vetera*.

Avery Cardinal Dulles, SJ (+2008), was the Laurence J. McGinley Professor of Religion and Society at Fordham University, a position he held from 1988 to 2008. Previously he taught at Woodstock College and The Catholic University of America, in addition to serving as visiting professor at many other eminent universities, including the Gregorian University, the University of Notre Dame, and Yale University. The author of over 750 articles on theological topics, Cardinal Dulles published over 20 books displaying his extraordinary theological competence and range, among them *Models of the Church*, *Models of Revelation*, *The Catholicity of the Church*, *The Craft of Theology*, *The Assurance of Things Hoped For*, *The Splendor of Faith: The Theological Vision of Pope John Paul II*, *The New World of Faith*, *Newman*, *The History of Apologetics*, and *Magisterium: Teacher and Guardian of the Faith*. Widely consulted for his theological acumen, he served on numerous ecumenical dialogues and on the International Theological Commission. He was named a Cardinal of the Catholic Church by Pope John Paul II.

Joseph W. Koterski, SJ, is Professor of Philosophy at Fordham University, where he has served as Chair of the Department of Philosophy. Previously he taught at St. Louis University. Since 1994 he has served as Editor-in-Chief of *International Philosophical Quarterly*. With Romanus Cessario, he is co-editor of Fordham University Press's Series in Moral Philosophy and Theology. In addition to numerous scholarly and popular articles, he is the author of *An Introduction* *to Medieval Philosophy: Basic Concepts*. He has co-edited many books, including *Prophecy and Diplomacy: The Moral Teaching of Pope John Paul II*, *Karl Jaspers on Philosophy of History and History of Philosophy*, and *The Two Wings of Catholic Thought: Essays on Fides et Ratio*. He is a member of the Board of Directors of the University Faculty for Life. At Fordham University, he has received both the Undergraduate Teaching Award and the Graduate Teacher of the Year Award.

Matthew Levering is Associate Professor of Theology at the University of Dayton, and has also served as the Myser Fellow at the Center for Ethics and Culture at the University of Notre Dame. He is the co-editor of *Nova et Vetera*. He is the author of *Christ's Fulfillment of Torah and Temple*, *Scripture and Metaphysics*, *Sacrifice and Community*, *Participatory Biblical Exegesis*, *Biblical Natural Law*, and *Ezra and Nehemiah*. His *Christ and the Catholic Priesthood: Ecclesial Hierarchy and the Pattern of the Trinity* is forthcoming from Hillenbrand Books. With Matthew L. Lamb, he co-edited *Vatican II: Tradition within Renewal*. He serves as co-editor for three book series. Currently he is co-editing *The Oxford Handbook on the Trinity* with Gilles Emery, OP.

Bruce D. Marshall is Professor of Historical Theology at Perkins School of Theology at Southern Methodist University. Prior to this, he taught at St. Olaf College. In addition to numerous influential articles, he is the author of *Trinity and Truth* and *Christology in Conflict: The Identity of a Saviour in Rahner and Barth*. He edited *Theology and Dialogue: Essays in Conversation with George Lindbeck*. Currently he is working on two books, a study of Aquinas on Christ and Israel and a collection of essays on Aquinas's theology.

Robert C. Miner is Associate Professor of Philosophy in the Honors College at Baylor University. Previously he taught at Boston College and Xavier University. In addition to numerous articles and reviews, his books include *Vico: Genealogist of Modernity*, *Truth in the Making: Creative Knowledge in Theology and Philosophy*, and *Aquinas on the Passions: A Study of Summa Theologiae I-II qq. 22–48*.

About the Liturgical Institute

The Liturgical Institute, founded in 2000 by His Eminence Francis Cardinal George of Chicago, offers a variety of options for education in liturgical studies. A unified, rites-based core curriculum constitutes the foundation of the program, providing integrated and balanced studies toward the advancement of the renewal promoted by the Second Vatican Council. The musical, artistic, and architectural dimensions of worship are given particular emphasis in the curriculum. Institute students are encouraged to participate in its "liturgical heart" of daily Mass and Morning and Evening Prayer. The academic program of the Institute serves a diverse, international student population—laity, religious, and clergy—who are preparing for service in parishes, dioceses, and religious communities. Personalized mentoring is provided in view of each student's ministerial and professional goals. The Institute is housed on the campus of the University of St. Mary of the Lake/Mundelein Seminary, which offers the largest priestly formation program in the United States and is the center of the permanent diaconate and lay ministry training programs of the Archdiocese of Chicago. In addition, the University has the distinction of being the first chartered institution of higher learning in Chicago (1844), and one of only seven pontifical faculties in North America.

For more information about the Liturgical Institute and its programs, contact: usml.edu/liturgicalinstitute. Phone: 847-837-4542. E-mail: litinst@usml.edu.

Msgr. Reynold Hillenbrand
1904-1979

Monsignor Reynold Hillenbrand, ordained a priest by Cardinal George Mundelein in 1929, was Rector of St. Mary of the Lake Seminary from 1936 to 1944.

He was a leading figure in the liturgical and social action movement in the United States during the 1930s and worked to promote active, intelligent, and informed participation in the Church's liturgy.

He believed that a reconstruction of society would occur as a result of the renewal of the Christian spirit, whose source and center is the liturgy.

Hillenbrand taught that, since the ultimate purpose of Catholic action is to Christianize society, the renewal of the liturgy must undoubtedly play the key role in achieving this goal.

Hillenbrand Books strives to reflect the spirit of Monsignor Reynold Hillenbrand's pioneering work by making available innovative and scholarly resources that advance the liturgical and sacramental life of the Church.